What do you do when your kids say . . .

"MOMMY, THERE'S NOTHING TO DO!"

Instead of planting them in front of the TV set again, why don't you ask them to write a review of their favorite show?

Instead of digging through those dusty, broken toys again, why don't you show them how to make some new ones using common household items?

Instead of thinking up chores for them to do, why don't you put them to work making their own greeting cards for the holidays?

There are plenty of creative ways to keep your kids occupied—without expensive toys and time-consuming work. Turn bored children into busy children—with MOMMY, THERE'S NOTHING TO DO!

Most Berkley Books are available at special quantity discounts for bulk purchases for sales promotions, premiums, fund raising, or educational use. Special books or book excerpts can also be created to fit specific needs.

For details, write or telephone Special Markets, The Berkley Publishing Group, 200 Madison Avenue, New York, New York 10016; (212) 951-8800.

Mommy, There's Nothing to Do!

How TO TURN BORED CHILDREN INTO BUSY CHILDREN

CYNTHIA MacGREGOR

BERKLEY BOOKS, NEW YORK

If you purchased this book without a cover, you should be aware that this book is stolen property. It was reported as "unsold and destroyed" to the publisher, and neither the author nor the publisher has received any payment for this "stripped book."

IMPORTANT REMINDER: Only parents can determine which activities are appropriate for their children, and the author and the publisher of this book encourage all parents to be careful in selecting and supervising their children to protect their health and safety. The author and publisher cannot accept any responsibility for inappropriate selection of activities for children based on age, physical ability or intelligence, or for unsupervised activities of any kind that could lead to injury.

MOMMY, THERE'S NOTHING TO DO!

A Berkley Book / published by arrangement with
the author

PRINTING HISTORY
Berkley edition / September 1993

All rights reserved.
Copyright © 1993 by Cynthia MacGregor.
This book may not be reproduced in whole or in part,
by mimeograph or any other means, without permission.
For information address: The Berkley Publishing Group,
200 Madison Avenue, New York, New York 10016.

ISBN: 0-425-13911-5

BERKLEY ®
Berkley Books are published by The Berkley Publishing Group,
200 Madison Avenue, New York, New York 10016.
BERKLEY and the "B" design
are trademarks belonging to Berkley Publishing Corporation.

PRINTED IN THE UNITED STATES OF AMERICA

For Laurel—may she use it well

Acknowledgments

The author greatly appreciates the contributions of the following people (in alphabetical order):

      Vic Bobb
      John Davidson
      Bill Franz
      Laurel Koesterich
      Sheryl Pease

Contents

Introduction	1
Games	3
The Arts	15
Holiday Activities	25
Homemade Toys	35
Educational Activities	55
Car Games	75
Arts & Crafts Projects	87
Miscellaneous Activities	133

Introduction

"MOMMY, THERE'S NOTHING to do!" If those aren't every parent's least-favorite words, they must rank pretty high on the list. What do you do when your child or children voice this old, familiar complaint? Turn on the "electronic baby-sitter" and hope to find something educational? Launch into a list of toys that are sitting, neglected, in the toy chest? Quietly pull your hair out? Stifle a scream?

In this book you'll find an assortment of activities suited primarily for children between the ages of three and ten, though some of the activities may interest their older brothers and sisters as well. Some of these activities are perfect for those times when you want to do something with the kids; others require no parental supervision and will keep the kids occupied while you balance the checkbook. Some are definitely games for more than one child at a time, others are activities that will keep only children occupied without siblings or friends needed; most are suitable for either one or more children.

I've divided the book into eight sections: Games, The Arts, Holiday Activities, Homemade Toys, Educational Activities, Car Games, Arts & Crafts Projects, and Miscellaneous Activities, but of course there are lots of crossovers. Holiday activities may be crafts, car games are often educational, and educational activities can be fun games.

Not surprisingly, Arts & Crafts Projects is the biggest section by far, and no wonder, since it encompasses everything from several kinds of painting to the making of simple jewelry of the sorts kids like. Don't worry if your child has ten thumbs. S/he doesn't have to be a creative genius to enjoy these activities.

Some of the pastimes in this book may be old friends: "Gee, I did that when *I* was a kid! I'd forgotten all about it." Others will undoubtedly be new to you. For sure, there's something here for every parent who has a child between the ages of three and ten.

Next time you hear, "Mommy, there's nothing to do!" you'll be ready with an answer!

Games

Flying Shuffleboard

MATERIALS NEEDED: *Cardboard box or several boxes, scissors, markers, string or rope*

FLYING SHUFFLEBOARD CAN be played indoors or out, though it's ideal as a backyard activity for one or more children. The materials are no-cost, and the kids get enjoyment out of making the game pieces themselves before play ever starts.

Each child cuts seven pieces from a cardboard box. They can be squares, triangles, ovals, or circles, and can be anywhere from five inches in diameter to dinner-plate-sized. Each child marks his/her pieces with a distinctive color or design, to identify them. It is important that each player be able to distinguish his/her own pieces.

The playing field can be any area, indoors or out, that allows the participants the chance to stand ten to twenty feet away. Lay out the rope or string in four concentric circles, with the center circle being perhaps a foot in diameter. The actual size will depend on the space available and on how easy you want to make the game for the players.

Players stand behind a line of string or rope to skim their pieces at the circles. How far back you place the string line will depend on how old the kids are and how far they can throw. They take turns flipping or skimming their pieces toward the target, aiming for the center circle.

The simple backhanded flip motion that's used to

throw a Frisbee is the most predictable and efficient throw for getting these pieces into the circle, but of course the kids can feel free to experiment with any approach that works for them.

Scoring: Give each player 10 points for each piece that lands in the center circle, 9 for each piece in the circle around it, 8 for the circle around that, and 7 for the circle around that. Pieces that land on parts of two circles get scored the higher of the two possible scores. In other words, it is not necessary for the piece to land entirely within the confines of the bull's-eye for it to score 10 points. The first player to score 100 points wins the game.

What's Missing?

MATERIALS NEEDED: *Tray or platter, dish towel or piece of similar fabric, any ten different small items such as a button, nail file, pencil, small ball, coin, leaf, chestnut, marble, etc.*

THIS IS A game for two players. One player (most likely the parent) gathers ten small items from around the house and places them on the tray, covers all the items with the towel, then presents the tray to the other player (most likely the child). The tray is uncovered, allowing the player to look at the items for fifteen seconds before the tray is re-covered.

After the fifteen seconds, that player turns his/her back while the other player removes one item from the tray and hides it. The player whose back is turned then turns around again, looks at the tray, now uncovered, and tries to identify the missing item.

For a younger child, you can play with only five items. For an older child, you can make the assortment of items deliberately more confusing by making several of them similar. For instance, you can have two or three buttons of different colors, two or three coins of different denominations. You can also rearrange the order of the items on the tray to make identification and memorization more difficult.

I'm Thinking of Something

MATERIALS NEEDED: *None*

THIS VERSION OF Twenty Questions can be tailored to children of various age levels. It can be played by two or more players, and among kids only or with parents participating.

The basic game simply involves one person announcing, "I'm thinking of something, and it starts with *F.*" For easy play among younger kids, there is no limit to the number of questions that may be asked. The kids can keep asking till they get the answer. The fun is in eventually deducing the right answer.

For older kids, the number of questions may be limited: If the questioner fails to guess the object correctly in, say, twenty-five questions, the person who's thinking of something wins; if the correct object is guessed, the questioner wins.

With more than two players, the questioners take turns asking, and the one who guesses right first wins.

For older players, you can make a rule that if you guess an actual object and you're wrong, you're out of the game.

Though kids think this is just a fun game, it really is educational, too. Many cognitive skills are sharpened by this contest of wits. For instance, even if you're not playing that a wrong guess about an actual object will put you out of the game, kids soon learn that it's not advantageous to guess actual objects early in the game. "Is it my cat?" is not nearly as helpful as "Is it alive?" "Is it in this room?" "Is it bigger than me?"

For really little kids or beginners, further clues may be given at the outset: "I'm thinking of someone you know and their name begins with *M*." "I'm thinking of an animal and it starts with *D*." Even children too young to know their alphabet well can play: "I'm thinking of something in this room and it's blue."

Parents should remember that the learning aspect of the game—and it adds to the fun, too—is in the child coming to realize what kind of questions elicit the most useful information. They learn to use their deductive processes as they learn to ask questions like, "Is it something Grandma has at her house?" "Is it something you can eat?" "Is it in this room?" "Is it part of the body?"

A good game at any time, this can be played at the drop of a hat, with no preparations, and in a car as well as in a house, in the park, or in virtually any location. It's equally suitable, too, for playing with parents or just among the kids.

Which Hand?

MATERIALS NEEDED: *Coin or any other small object*

THIS GAME IS great fun for really small children, who will be happy to guess over and over which hand the coin is in. It's simple enough: The parent (or other child) holds both hands out toward the child, with the coin or other small object resting on one palm. This player then makes hand-washing motions, ending up with two clenched fists, the coin hidden in one of them. Holding out both hands, s/he says, "Guess which hand it's in?"

That's all there is to it, but for a small child it's plenty, and most enjoyable.

Rhyme Game

MATERIALS NEEDED: *Pencil and several sheets of paper*

THE PARENT CHOOSES a word and asks the child to come up with as many words as possible that rhyme with that word. As the child mentions appropriate words, the parent writes them down.

If the child is not familiar with the concept of making up rhymes (poems) such as nursery rhymes, the parent should recite a couple of them to the child, pointing out how the words at the ends of the lines rhyme. Then the parent can ask the child to develop his/her own rhyme, using some of the rhyming words s/he has just come up with.

Alphabet House

MATERIALS NEEDED: *Pencil and paper*

ALPHABET HOUSE IS educational as well as fun, being an alphabet game that will help familiarize the child with his/her letters. It is also suitable for older children who already know their letters. It can be played by just one child, as a challenge rather than a competitive game, simply trying to fill out his/her list from *A* to *Z*, the challenge being to complete the task. Or it can be played by more than one child, the object being to be the first to complete his/her list.

With small children who cannot yet write, the parent will have to go around with the child to do the writing-down; older kids can go around the house on their own.

The child or children's task is to find something in the house that begins with each letter of the alphabet. *A* can be *apple* or *aluminum pan*; *B* can be *book* or *bottle,* and so forth. If this proves too easy, ask for *two* items beginning with each letter. For further fun, if the kids have had a good time but have already filled up their lists from *A* to *Z*, ask them to go around the house again, this time looking for objects that *end* with the letters from *A* to *Z*.

If you think the kids are going to be too frustrated by *Q*, *X*, and *Z*, you can tell the kids to just draw a picture of something beginning with that letter or omit it entirely. But if they have a toy xylophone and a toy zebra, and if you have a deck of cards with a queen in it, the problem is solved.

Mirror Image

MATERIALS NEEDED: *One picture of a face cut from a magazine (in color), white drawing paper, crayons or pastels or colored markers, glue stick*

FIND A LARGE, full-face color photo in a magazine. (Makeup ads are very suitable for this.) Carefully cut the picture in half, draw a line down the center of a piece of white drawing paper, and glue the picture to the corresponding side of the center line. (In other words, if you are using the right half of the picture, place it on the right side; if using the left half, place it on the left of the center line.)

With crayons, pastels, or markers, the child now tries to draw a "mirror image," matching the hairline, eyes, nose, skin tone, and mouth next to the picture. The result will be interesting at the least and possibly quite comical.

Read Your Mind Number Game

MATERIALS NEEDED: *Number chart, which follows*

WITH THIS NIFTY math puzzle, people will think you can read their minds. They think of a number between one and sixty, and you'll be able to tell them what that number is! The first time you do it with your kids, of course they'll pick the number and you'll "read their minds." After a while of amazing them with it, you may want to explain how it works so they can have fun doing it with their friends.

Here's how to do it: After they pick a number, ask them to tell you which group or groups on the chart that number is located in. Then, simply look at the numbers in the top right-hand corners of the groups their number is in, add those numbers together, and tell them the number they were thinking of.

Example: Suppose they pick number fifty-seven. When you say to them, "Which groups is your number in?" they would answer, "Group one, group two, group four, and group six." You then add the numbers in the upper right corner of each group: eight, thirty-two, one, and sixteen, which totals fifty-seven, their number.

Not only is this a fun trick—and what child doesn't like "magic"?—it offers valuable practice in addition. Once the kids know how to work the trick, they're going to want to do it themselves, often, and they'll be getting math practice every time.

The chart follows:

	Group One						Group Two				
9	10	11	12	13	8	33	34	35	36	37	32
14	15	24	25	26	27	38	39	40	41	42	43
28	29	30	31	40	41	44	45	46	47	48	49
42	43	44	45	46	47	50	51	52	53	54	55
56	57	58	59	60	13	56	57	58	59	60	46

	Group Three						Group Four				
3	6	7	10	11	2	3	5	7	9	11	1
14	15	18	19	22	23	13	15	17	19	21	23
26	27	30	31	34	35	25	27	29	31	33	35
38	39	42	43	46	47	37	39	41	43	46	47
50	51	54	55	58	59	49	51	53	55	57	59

	Group Five						Group Six				
5	6	7	13	12	4	17	18	19	20	21	16
14	15	20	21	22	23	22	23	24	25	26	27
28	29	30	31	36	37	28	29	30	31	48	49
38	39	44	45	46	47	50	51	52	53	54	55
52	53	54	55	60	13	56	57	58	59	60	16

Following Directions Test

MATERIALS NEEDED: *A typed sheet of paper (copy the instructions below) and a pencil*

FOR CHILDREN WHO are able to read, this is a fun game that teaches the child the importance of following directions. Parents should type out the following set of instructions (beginning with the title, below) and present the typed sheet to their reading-age children. Then stand back and wait for realization to set in.

Afterward, the kids will have fun pulling this stunt on their friends.

Give the kids the typed sheet and a pencil, and tell them it's a fun test, and they're to follow the directions in it.

Can You Follow Directions?

This is a timed test. You have five minutes to complete it.

1. Read everything carefully before doing anything.
2. Write your name in the upper right-hand corner of this page.
3. Circle the word *corner* in the second sentence.
4. Stand on your chair and act like an ape, making monkey noises.
5. Write your name in the air with your finger.
6. Draw a sun on the bottom of this page.
7. Put a big *X* over the sun you just drew.
8. Roll over and over on the floor and say, "I'm being silly," five times.
9. Completely circle instruction number 8.
10. Sing the theme song to your favorite TV show.
11. Draw a square, a triangle, and a circle in the upper left-hand corner of this page.
12. On the back of this page, add the numbers 2, 4, 23, and 42.
13. Loudly call out your first name—now!
14. Shout out, "I am nearly finished. I have followed the directions."
15. Now that you have finished reading everything carefully before doing anything, as instruction number 1 said, do only as instruction number 2 directs, and you're finished.

The Arts

Broadway-Bound

MATERIALS NEEDED: None, except for possible props for the play and a video camera if you have one

KIDS OF ANY age can write a simple little play and perform it for their friends or the other kids in the neighborhood. Never mind if it's only five or ten minutes long; the important thing is that they're involved, they're busy, they're being creative, they're exercising their imaginations, and they're having fun. It also gives them a chance to show off in a very positive way.

Optimally, the kids can both write and perform in the play, but if there's a child who's creative but shy, s/he can write the play without performing, and if there's a child who's outgoing but not especially creative, s/he can perform without participating in the actual writing. Most kids, however, can do both and will be happy to do so. Remember, we're not interested here in whether the script or acting will win a Tony Award, we're just out for everyone to have a good time.

Particularly creative kids can write their own original play; for the average child, suggest acting out a well-known story or a part of a favorite book or nursery rhyme. Older kids can sit down and write out a script, rehearse it before putting it on for an audience of parents and/or friends and/or siblings, and go all-out in the production. For younger kids or those less theatrically oriented, an impromptu, unrehearsed, improvised performance is fine.

Of course they can get really ambitious and do it with costumes, but ordinary clothes are fine, too. What's wrong with using a little imagination?!

If you have a video camera, by all means record the performance for posterity.

Wet and Wild Xylophone

MATERIALS NEEDED: *Eight small glasses or canning jars, water, fork, wooden spoon*

THIS SIMPLE ACTIVITY gives kids a chance to make "homemade music" while experimenting with different notes of the scale. Simply set the eight glasses or jars in a row on the table, filling each with a different amount of water. By carefully tapping the top of each glass with a fork, the kids will hear different musical notes. Older kids/musical perfectionists can adjust the amount of water in each glass till they have a perfect de-re-mi-fa-sol-la-ti-do, but for most kids, it's enough to have eight different notes emanating from the glasses.

Now, for a further experiment, have the kids tap the top of each glass with the wooden spoon and see what a different sound they get compared to tapping the glasses with the fork.

If the glasses have been filled with the correct amounts of water to provide all eight notes of the scale, the kids can now experiment and learn to play simple tunes like "Twinkle, Twinkle Little Star." Or they can make up their own tunes, which is also a good plan for kids whose glasses don't exactly conform to the eight notes of the scale.

If the glasses *do* represent the eight notes, a piece of tape affixed at the water level on each glass makes an easy guide as to how far to fill up each glass next time your kids want to play the wet and wild xylophone.

Write Commercials

MATERIALS NEEDED: *Paper and pen or pencil*

THE KIDS CAN have fun while stretching their imaginations and creativity by writing their own commercials for either real products or imaginary ones. If they're young and have never thought about commercials objectively before, explain exactly what a commercial is and what its job is. After they've written their commercials, you can get into a discussion with them of just how commercials persuade viewers to buy a product.

They may prefer to write the commercials down or just to act them out, or both. Chances are their commercials, and the products they may invent to advertise, will lean toward the silly. This is fine.

This activity will not only provoke their creativity but will also make them think about the factors at work on them when they watch commercials on TV.

Create a Book

MATERIALS NEEDED: Paper and pen or pencil, possibly construction paper

SPARK THE KIDS' creativity by getting them to write stories, which can eventually be turned into little homemade books. These can be either handwritten by the kids on white paper with construction-paper covers, if they're old enough, or dictated to you. If you want the book to look more like a real book, it can be typed by you or by a cooperative older sibling who types. If the kids enjoy drawing, they can provide illustrations for the book as well.

If your kids are particularly creative, they can make up stories of their own from scratch with no coaching. If they need a jump start, suggest any or all of the following projects.

1. Rewrite your favorite fairy tale or other story, telling it the way you think it *should* have happened.
2. Write a story about what happened to a fairy tale character after the end of the classic story. For example, what happened to the three pigs after the wolf fell down the chimney? Did the two lazy pigs learn their lesson? Did the Big Bad Wolf's hungry cousin come looking for them? What happened? Or take Cinderella: Did she and the prince have kids after they got married? What were their names? What kind of adventures did they have? And what

happened to the wicked stepsisters after Cinderella got married?
3. Rewrite any story, true or fictitious, as if it happened to you.
4. Write a short, fictitious story about yourself. Suggested topics:
   My Imaginary Pet
   When the Martians Came to Visit Me
   Robin Hood and I
5. Write a true story starring yourself and/or your friends. Suggested topics:
   My Best Friend and I
   The Best Thing About My Best Friend
   My Pet
   My Favorite Thing in the World
   The Most Fun I Ever Had
6. Write a poem. Any topic. Any length.
7. Make up some riddles

Telling Tales

MATERIALS NEEDED: *Magazine*

LOOK THROUGH A magazine with your child until s/he is attracted to a photograph in it. (Very likely the photo will be part of an advertisement. That's OK.) The point of the activity is for the child to use his or her imagination on the raw material of the photograph.

"Tell me about this man/woman," you'll ask the child. "What do you think his/her name might be? Now make up a story about him/her." If the child is slow to start, try to elicit the following information: What is the person in the picture doing? If there are other people in the picture, what might their relationship be to the main person in the picture? What might they have been doing right before the picture was taken? What do you suppose they're going to do next? Are they having fun?

Depending on the child's age, his/her degree of creativity and originality, and how much you want to provoke thought (as opposed to just letting this be an exercise in imagination), you might ask other questions, such as: "Do you suppose this woman has a job? Doing what? Does she remind you of anyone you know? Why? Do you think her kitchen would look like this if she lived in Nigeria? Russia?" You can even turn this activity into a chance to examine values if the child describes a scenario that lends itself to such a discussion.

There are virtually no age limits for this activity. Kids develop imaginations at an early age. Any age child can benefit from exercising the speculative, the imaginative, and the creative "muscles." If the child gets off to a slow start, you can always start making up a story yourself, then stop and ask the child to take over. You can even take turns, writing alternating chapters with your child: first your turn, then his/hers, then yours, etc. The story can be dramatic, comic, absurd, or just plain silly.

This pastime also works as a time-passer on a car trip. And it's entirely possible that this exercise might turn out to be among the earliest imaginative activities of a budding writer. This was the case with one of the contributors to this book!

Be a Critic

MATERIALS NEEDED: *Paper and pencil or pen*

IF THE KIDS insist on watching TV (and we all know they will), challenge their critical senses and spark their creativity by asking them to write reviews of some of the shows they watch. If they're not familiar with the format or premise of a review, read them a movie review from your local paper. Now have them sit down and write reviews of selected TV shows. This also works with movies they have seen, whether on TV, in the theater, or on rented video cassettes.

Remember, the dual objectives are to get them to think about what they're watching and to get them to be creative, so praise their efforts if they're at all insightful and/or creative, and by all means have a discussion of the show and of their review of it, after they've read it aloud.

Rhythm Sticks

MATERIALS NEEDED: *Two sticks, preferably eighteen-inch dowels, and recorded music*

TAKE TWO STICKS or, if possible, cut wooden dowels into eighteen-inch lengths. Put on some music that is familiar to the child and have the child play along with the other musicians by softly hitting the dowels together in rhythm to the music.

Once the child has mastered finding the beat, more elaborate rhythms can be attempted such as hitting the sticks together on the off beat, or hitting them together double time.

Holiday Activities

Birthday Cloth

MATERIALS NEEDED: *Solid-colored twin sheet (white or pastel), permanent color markers, newspapers, masking tape*

THIS IS AN activity for a birthday party (or, for that matter, a party for any other occasion as well). When the kids have had enough of Pin the Tail and whatever other games you've planned, offer them a chance to have fun and be creative in a different way. Here's an activity they may not have taken part in at anyone else's party.

Spread newspapers on the floor where the birthday party guests will be working on the cloth to prevent the colors from bleeding through and staining the floor. Place the sheet on top of the newspapers and secure it firmly to the floor with masking tape.

Ask each child to draw something on the cloth and sign his/her name and age. Since the markers dry quickly, the cloth can be used for a tablecloth when the food, ice cream, and cake are served. After the party, the cloth can safely be washed in cold water and put away for the following year, when more drawings, names, and ages can be added to it. It makes a nice keepsake, and after the first year or two, children can look back at the number of friends they've kept through the years.

For kids too young to draw at all well, you can trace their hands or feet and write in their names and ages.

Candy Cane Reindeer Ornaments

MATERIALS NEEDED: *Wrapped candy canes, brown pipe cleaners, glue-on plastic eyes, small red pom-poms, glue*

THESE QUICK AND easy ornaments will add a charming touch to your Christmas tree, and they're so simple that even very young children will be able to successfully construct them with just a little help.

Procedure: The reindeer's body is a candy cane, with a pipe cleaner providing the antlers. Bend a long pipe cleaner in half and twist it around the top of the candy cane. The cane will appear to be hanging from the pipe cleaner. Now bend the pipe cleaner to resemble antlers. You may even wish to add shorter pieces to make the antlers branch out.

Next glue the eyes on, and then the nose, which is the pom-pom, and goes on the front of the candy cane. You now have a completed reindeer, ready to hang on the tree in the same manner you would have before it was decorated.

Quilted Tree Ornaments

***

MATERIALS NEEDED: Styrofoam balls, scraps of material (cotton and/or cotton-polyester, small print and/or solid color), nail file, quarter-inch ribbon or pipe cleaners

THESE EXCEPTIONALLY ATTRACTIVE ornaments allow even the crafts novice to produce professional-appearing decorations. Since uniformity of size and exactness of shape are not necessary, a child old enough to use a scissors can get it right even if his/her cutting isn't perfect. But since a scissors and a nail file are involved, the child should be old enough to handle both with respect, or else parental assistance is called for.

Procedure: The fabric scraps should be cut into roughly circular or oval pieces a couple of inches in diameter. Lay one of the pieces of fabric on one Styrofoam ball. Placing the tip of the nail file about a quarter-inch in from the edge of the fabric, press the cloth down into the Styrofoam, working all the way around the edge in this fashion, till the whole piece is melded into the ball.

Select another piece of cloth and lay it on the ball so that a portion of its edge overlaps a portion of the already-installed cloth, and then repeat the edge-embedding procedure, pushing the second piece into the same groove into which the original was pushed.

As your child gains experience in covering the entire ball with varicolored and multipatterned cloth, s/he will want to experiment with the different effects that can be achieved either by juxtaposing strikingly different colors or patterns, or by coordinating complementary tones.

The hanger for the ball can be as simple as a piece of pipe cleaner pushed down into the foam and bent into a hook at the other end, or it can be as elegant as a six- to eight-inch strip of quarter-inch ribbon formed into a hanging loop by having its ends pushed gently into the styrofoam by the nail file.

Be warned: This activity is fun, and even if your intention is to let the kids work on this one alone, you're likely to get drawn into making these ornaments yourself, along with them. Be further warned: A couple of casual tree-ornament-makers in the Midwest became so enchanted by the impressive, rich-looking quilted balls they were producing that they wound up going into business.

Handprint Wrapping Paper

MATERIALS NEEDED: Paint (tempera, fingerpaint, or homemade finger paint—see page 40 of this book), paper (butcher paper, blank newsprint, or brown grocery-bag paper will do fine)

FOLKS ARE SURE to treasure the wrapping paper as much as the contents of the gift when the paper features the unique and inimitable handprint of their own child, grandchild, niece, or nephew.

The procedure is simplicity itself: The child paints his/her palm and fingers with tempera or fingerpaint, then presses the image of the hand onto the paper destined to wrap Grandma's next present.

Options include a piece containing precisely one handprint, paper marked by the child's handprints in various colors, or paper that the child has uniquely decorated in some other way. It is possible to have more than one child handprint the paper, with each using his/her own color and signing his/her name under the handprint.

It's simple, inexpensive, and it's treasured by the recipient. Best of all, it's fun.

Lace Easter Eggs

MATERIALS NEEDED: *Round balloons, string or embroidery floss, all-purpose glue, spray paint (if desired), pie tin, newspaper or similar covering to work on. Optional: Easter grass, small figurines such as rabbits or chicks. Also optional: Oatmeal carton or similar round container, and paint, paper, or fabric scraps to decorate it with*

THIS IS A fun activity to keep children busy during rainy spring weekends and the portion of Easter vacation that falls before the actual holiday.

Procedure: Spread the newspaper to protect your work surface. Now blow up the balloons. Pour glue into the pie pan and immerse long pieces of string in the glue, making sure the string is well covered with the glue. Carefully take the string out of the glue, letting the excess drip off. Spread the glued string on the balloon, making a lacy pattern. Repeat until the balloon is covered in an attractive design.

Let the glue dry, then pop the balloon. If desired, carefully cut an opening in the front of the "egg" and add easter grass and small figurines. Or leave the egg whole. Either way, these eggs make attractive decorations, and the kids have the satisfaction of being able to say, "I made them myself."

If desired, you can cut a small oatmeal carton or other round container in half, decorate it with paper, paint, or fabric scraps, and use it as a stand for your egg.

This project also can be undertaken as a Christmas ball project, with the balloons blown up smaller than the Easter egg balloons. After the balloons are blown up and decorated with string, they can be spray-painted with holiday colors or glitter paint.

Homemade Greeting Cards

MATERIALS NEEDED: *Paper, pencil, crayons or markers*

HANDMADE, PERSONALIZED GREETING cards are a double gift: They give parents the gift of some quiet time while the kids are working on them, and then they give the recipients the gift of a thoughtful, personalized greeting from the child.

Kids may need to be coaxed to convey birthday greetings over the phone. ("Please get on the phone and wish Grandma happy birthday."—"I don't wanna.") But most kids jump at the chance to get artistic and draw Grandma (or whoever) a homemade, personalized, all-their-own greeting. ("The nicest gift you could give Grandma would be a card you made all by yourself."—"Where are my crayons?")

While younger children are usually delighted simply to fill a sheet of paper with a picture and perhaps a few words, if they can write, older kids will probably want their efforts to resemble commercial greeting cards. By folding a piece of typing paper in half from the top down, then folding that half sheet in half again from left to right, they'll have just the right size and shape, with an outside and an inside. A picture on the outside and the greeting on the inside will suffice, though older and more creative card makers may work hard to devise messages that begin on the outside and continue on the inside.

In addition to giving the child a project to occupy his/her time, saving on money at the greeting card store, and providing the recipient with a personalized greeting, making cards can provide an opportunity for parent and child to engage in a serious discussion about the meaning of holidays, about customs and rituals, about the value of friends and family, and about the practices of conventional courtesy.

Holiday Place Mats

MATERIALS NEEDED: 8" × 12" drawing paper (or heavyweight 8½" × 11" typing paper), crayons, clear adhesive paper (18" width)

THIS CRAFT CAN be adapted to almost any holiday or occasion, from Christmas to birthdays to big sister's return home from college or older brother's graduation from high school.

Procedure: Draw on the paper the picture or words or both that you wish to have on the place mat. It can be a Christmas or snow scene, a jack o'lantern for Halloween, the words "WELCOME HOME," the words "HAPPY BIRTHDAY" with a picture of a candle or cake, or whatever suits the occasion (and is within the child's ability). Use bold, bright colors to draw with.

Leaving the backing on the adhesive paper, cut two 18" × 10" pieces. Place one of these flat on the table, backing side up, and carefully remove the backing. Now center the drawing above the adhesive, design side down. Carefully place the drawing on the adhesive paper, pressing from center to edges to eliminate air bubbles or wrinkles.

Place the second piece of adhesive paper, backing side up, on the table, and remove the backing. Carefully place the first piece, with the drawing on it, on top of this, so that the back of the drawing is facing the adhesive. Having sandwiched the drawing between the two pieces of adhesive paper, repeat the smoothing process with the second sheet of adhesive paper, pressing from center to edges to eliminate air bubbles or wrinkles.

(For younger children, it may be necessary for the parent to take care of the adhesive-paper aspect of this operation, after the kids get done doing the drawing.)

Now take a scissors and trim away the excess adhesive paper carefully, leaving a one-inch border around the drawing.

These place mats can be used repeatedly, from one Christmas, birthday, or whatever to the next, as they can easily be wiped clean with a damp cloth.

Variations: Instead of drawing a picture, cut out magazine pictures or filled-in pictures from a coloring book, or even photographs, and glue these to the piece of drawing paper. You can even make a collage of cut-up old birthday cards or Christmas cards, though anything with an uneven surface will present a bumpier place mat for balancing a plate on, so careful layering is recommended.

Homemade Toys

Handkerchief Parachute

MATERIALS NEEDED: *Large cotton handkerchief, string, and a weight (this can be any object weighing several ounces that is relatively easy to tie a string around, such as a heavy metal washer or several lighter ones, a small toy soldier, a pill bottle filled with sand, or anything else that will serve the same purpose)*

THIS CLASSIC TOY is easy to make, and as with all homemade toys, the pleasure of making it and the pride of having done so add greatly to the enjoyment of playing with it.

Procedure: Cut four pieces of string into identical lengths. Ordinary white cotton string is the best, and twelve to fourteen inches is the best length to cut it. Lay the hankie on the desk, spread out. The bigger the hankie, the better; one of those bandana-style handkerchiefs about eighteen inches on a side is ideal. Tie a string to each corner of the hankie, tying the knot about an inch in from the corner; a bunched-up little tail of cloth will puff out from the knot.

Put the four corners of the handkerchief together, trying to make sure that the strings are still roughly the same length. Grasp the ends of the strings together and, about four inches up from the ends, tie a fat knot.

The weight—toy soldier, washer, or whatever—is to be attached to these four loose string tails. Here's the advantage to the items suggested as weights; a rock or a chestnut is a good weight, too, but is hard to attach securely. However, that's not to say you have to limit yourself to the above suggestions. You may have any of a number of other odd items around the house, garage, or workshop that weigh several ounces and can easily be tied to the parachute strings. Feel free to be creative.

Now that the 'chute is ready to be played with, it's time to experiment with the best means of tossing it. Toss it up gently and you don't get a very long or exciting ride down; but at least the parachute gets up to the top of the arc of the throw and comes back. Exert all your strength and toss it as high as you can, and you'll get greater height; but the parachute might open on the way up.

For a child who doesn't frustrate easily, experimenting with different ways to toss the 'chute can be half the fun. For a child who does frustrate easily, a little parental guidance may be in order. There are four basic maneuvers for sending the handkerchief parachute into the air. You may want to try all four before deciding which works best.

1. Hold the parachute upside down in the palm of your hand, with the weight in your other hand, higher than the cloth. Lower the string and weight carefully into the middle of the cloth. Bunch it all together tightly, then throw the whole thing as high as possible.

    The good aspects of this system are that the 'chute gets good height and rarely opens on the way up. The bad aspect is that sometimes it doesn't open on the way down, either!

2. Hold the parachute in the center of the kerchief, (the top of the 'chute), so that all four corners are together. Swing the weight and string in increasingly speedy vertical circles (that is, imitating the motion of a ferris wheel), round and round, till the weight is whistling.

    Let go while the weight is on the upswing. (This takes some practice, and is best done when there is not another person right next to you. If you mis-

throw, the parachute and weight could fly sideways and hit a bystander. But, as it is light, it won't travel too far.) The speeding weight shoots upward, with the chute behind it. At the height of its flight, it curves back toward the ground, the 'chute opens, and the whole thing drifts gently down. The advantage: terrific height, if it works right. The disadvantage: If the 'chute opens on the way up, the whole flight comes to a sudden and shuddery end.
3. Hold the weight in your right hand, and hold the 'chute directly above it in your left hand. (For a lefty, reverse the positions.) Lower the string and cloth toward, and then over, the weight. Imagine a parachutist standing on the ground with his or her 'chute drifting directly down on top of him or her; that's what you wind up with here. Then toss the weight and 'chute upward, underhand. The advantages are that the 'chute rarely pops open on the way up, and almost always opens properly on the way down, giving a good ride. The disadvantage is that it's hard to get a lot of height with this method.
4. Chute and weight are carried into the sky by a "booster rocket," a missile of some sort that will detach itself and allow the parachute to descend freely. One fine means of boosting the parachute into the air is a softball. Balance the parachute on top of the softball, hold the ball from underneath, and aim for the sky. (Obviously this is a strictly outdoors method, not for indoor play.) When this works properly, it's one of the best methods for achieving great height. But when your throw is off, the ball doesn't go where it's supposed to, or the parachute falls off the ball early, you have a failed parachute ride and/or a lost ball to chase.

Of course, with a child old enough to safely lean out a window or climb a tree, the 'chute can be dropped from on high and watched from above as it slowly wafts to the ground.

Jigsaw Puzzles

MATERIALS NEEDED: Scissors, old magazines, glue, light-gauge cardboard (old file folders are ideal)

ONE NICE ASPECT of this activity, as with many other homemade toys, is that not only does making the toy keep the child busy for a while, but s/he is left with a toy that will be fun to play with on many subsequent occasions.

Have your child look through the magazines till s/he finds an appealing picture. (Ads are fine.) This is what s/he'll be turning into a puzzle.

Procedure: After cutting the picture out, carefully glue it to a piece of cardboard or tagboard, trimming the cardboard to match the size of the picture.

Once the glue has dried, cut the picture into pieces. The complexity of the cutting and of the patterns of cuts will depend on the child's age and ability to put together a jigsaw puzzle more than on his or her ability to cut. The parent can always help with the cutting, but neither participant wants to wind up creating a puzzle too complicated for the child to enjoy working on.

One way to cut patterns is to turn the cardboard over, draw a series of lines, semicircles, shapes, and swoops on the back, irrespective of the picture on the front, and then cut along the lines. The first time the kids do this, they may need parental help in designing the cut-out shapes, but once they get the hang of it, older kids should be fine on their own and even somewhat younger kids should be able to cut out simpler patterns.

You can compound the complexity of the puzzle-solving by cutting out several pictures, making jigsaw puzzles of all of them, and then mixing the pieces together. Now you have to sort as well as put the pieces together. (Hint: To minimize the frustration factor, give yourself a clue by color coding the puzzles. A spot of red on the back of each piece of one puzzle, a spot of green on the back of each piece of the next puzzle, and so on, can help eventually sort out which pieces go together when you're ready to give up.)

Old Christmas cards provide another source of pictures for homemade jigsaw puzzles, and because of the heavy stock on which cards are printed, they don't have to be pasted on cardboard before being cut apart. Since cards are smaller than most magazine pictures, you may want to cut smaller pieces in order to maintain the complexity of the puzzle.

Homemade Fingerpaints

MATERIALS NEEDED: 2 cups water, 4 tablespoons cornstarch, food coloring, paper to paint on (butcher paper or newsprint is as fine as any other paper)

FINGERPAINTING IS AMONG the favorite activities of many children, but commercially produced fingerpaints are expensive, and it is much more fun, anyhow, to make your own! If the kids aren't old enough to be around the stove by themselves, you can work on this project together.

Procedure: To 2 cups of water in a saucepan, add 4 tablespoons of cornstarch. Bring to a boil, stirring constantly till all the lumps are gone. As the mixture cools, pour into as many separate bowls as you wish to have colors. Now add a few drops of food coloring to each bowl, mix, adding more if needed till the desired shades are reached. Of course you can mix colors, such as red and blue to get purple.

These fingerpaints can be stored in the refrigerator, covered with plastic wrap, after being partially used.

The only problem is that the kids are going to produce so many masterpieces that you'll run out of wall and fridge space to display them.

Salt Clay

MATERIALS NEEDED: *1 cup flour, 1/3 cup salt, 1/3–1/2 cup water, mixing bowl. Optional: Food coloring, rolling pin, cookie cutter*

WHAT WE SAID about the fingerpaints is true here, too: Commercially produced clay is a great deal more expensive than the homemade variety, and making their own is a fun activity for the kids, anyhow.

Procedure: Mix flour and salt in a mixing bowl, adding water till the mixture is about the texture of bread dough. (The purpose of the salt is to keep the clay from being too sticky.) The clay can be tinted with food coloring if desired, though most kids won't care about the color.

This clay can be used like any ceramic clay, worked and shaped into figures or into bowls, ashtrays, doll dishes, or whatever your imagination can come up with. It can also be rolled out with a rolling pin and cut into shapes with a cookie cutter. Either way, when the clay dries, it's finished and ready—or ready to be painted, if desired.

Unused portions of the clay can be kept covered in the refrigerator for about a week.

Marshmallow Building Blocks

MATERIALS NEEDED: Box of round toothpicks, bag of miniature marshmallows. Optional: Paper or plastic drinking straws, large marshmallows

IF YOUR CHILD can resist the urge to eat this particular toy, you'll find your budding architects and engineers producing extraordinary structures.

Procedure: The marshmallows are used in lieu of the round connectors in a building blocks set, and the toothpicks join one marshmallow to the next. For more ambitious projects, you can incorporate large marshmallows and drinking straws, which can be cut to the desired lengths.

With just these as building materials, you can construct bridges, houses and apartment buildings, office buildings, vehicles, animals, and people. Marshmallows do harden, as anyone who's left a bowl of them out overnight has found out. But while this is a bad thing for marshmallows destined for the stomach, it's a good quality when it comes to marshmallow toys.

Impromptu Fort or Playhouse

MATERIALS NEEDED: A flat (not contoured) bed sheet, a table. Optional: Pillows

AN OLD SHEET and a table combine to equal hours of rainy day fun. Simply cover the table with the sheet so three sides are enclosed and one side is open for a fort, or so that all four sides are enclosed for a house. Pillows inside are great for sitting on if the kids want furniture inside their house.

If the sheet is old and dispensable, it can be drawn on with markers to simulate a fort, house, or even tepee. Doors can be cut into the side, and windows can be either drawn on the sheet or cut out.

When the kids are tired of playing fort or house, they can get cozy inside, talk, sing, and munch on lunch or popcorn. It's even a great spot for a nap!

Paper Airplanes

MATERIALS NEEDED: *Rectangular sheet(s) of paper. Optional: Paper clips*

WHEN'S THE LAST time you flew a paper airplane? Have your kids ever tried it? We bet you'll be hooked and join in with them in folding and flying these homemade aircraft! You can even build competing fleets and have an air war, or a race to see whose planes fly the farthest.

In case you've forgotten how to construct one of these aircraft, here's how to do it: Fold a rectangular sheet of paper in half lengthwise. Fold back one corner so its edge is even with the lengthwise fold, and fold back the facing corner in the same manner. Now fold down the entire length of both sides in half, and you have a paper airplane.

Of course, part of the fun is experimenting with different folds and trying to come up with a craft that flies better and farther.

Clipping two paper clips to the bottom, one at each end, may provide stabilization.

The airplanes can even be colored (draw windows, doors, an insignia), if desired.

Mixies

MATERIALS NEEDED: *Scissors, old magazines, glue, light-gauge cardboard (old file folders are ideal)*

THE FIRST TIME around, you'll want to prepare this activity in advance for your kids. After that, they may want to do it all themselves. Start by cutting out a dozen or so full-length pictures of people from magazine pictures and ads. The more different the pictures are, the better. Look for as many as possible recognizable role types (grandma, baby-sitter), people in uniform (firefighter, baseball player), and other defining pictures, as opposed to generic men, women, and kids. Try for some relative uniformity in the size of the pictures. After gluing the pictures to the cardboard and letting the glue dry, divide each figure into three pieces, making a horizontal cut at the neck and another at the waist of each person.

Now reassemble the pictures on a flat surface, making ludicrous match-ups. A grandmother's head may appear over a policeman's body over a little kid's legs, a businessman's head over a woman's body over a football player's legs, and so forth.

Little kids are usually delighted with the ridiculous effects achieved by playing mix-and-match with the pictures. After you've laid the pictures out in silly togetherness, the kids can have fun rearranging the body parts to make different but equally laughable match-ups. Somewhat older kids may want to treat the pieces as if they were a jigsaw puzzle and try to match the original body parts with each other, as if to solve a puzzle.

Shoe Box Train

MATERIALS NEEDED: *Three shoe boxes, yarn, sharp-pointed scissors or other implement for punching holes in the boxes*

A CHILD YOUNG enough to enjoy this toy will probably be too young to use a sharp-pointed hole-punching implement, so this is a toy you should plan on constructing with your child, rather than one you can turn him/her loose on to work on all on his/her own.

Remove the lids from the three shoe boxes. Punch a small hole near the bottom in the middle of each end of two boxes. Punch a similar hole at just one end of the remaining box. Thread the end of a twelve-inch length of yarn into each hole in one of the boxes with two holes in it. Knot the end of each piece of yarn inside the box, large enough that the yarn won't come out of the box. Now thread each piece of yarn through a hole in one of the two remaining boxes, knotting those ends as well, so that you have three boxes in a row, connected together by yarn. There should be at least six inches of yarn between each of the boxes.

One of your end boxes still has a hole in it with no yarn through it. Thread a two-foot length of yarn through that hole, so the child can pull the train. The train is now ready to be pulled around the house by your young engineer, possibly loaded with toys or small dolls if s/he wishes to make it more realistic by carrying passengers or freight.

Magic Gardens of Jupiter

MATERIALS NEEDED: *2 tablespoons liquid bluing, salt, disposable aluminum pie pan, piece of coal or charcoal briquet. Optional: Food coloring*

COMMERCIALLY AVAILABLE "MOON rocks" or "magic rocks" are simply variations on this old-time make-it-at-home project, which will grow unpredictable and unique formations that are breathtaking in their fragility and delicate beauty. You and your kids can have fun with this one, and the results are never quite the same from one time to the next.

Procedure: Into 2 tablespoons of bluing mix enough salt to produce a mixture the consistency of a very thick, grainy liquid. It should be the thickness of the water-and-sand mixture you'd dribble to make the fancy parts of a sand castle.

Place the coal or charcoal briquet in the middle of a disposable aluminum pie plate. Dribble the salt-and-bluing mix onto the coal, trying to keep the mix from running into the bottom of the pie plate as much as possible. You want most of it to remain on top of the coal. Carefully add water to the pie plate, being careful that the water doesn't touch or wash away the dribbles on top of the coal.

Within an hour, your Magic Gardens of Jupiter will begin to grow. Fantastical shapes and spires and puffy clumps will spread and climb. Since the growth is unpredictable, don't place the pan on a good, finished wood surface. And, since your Magic Garden of Jupiter is very delicate, almost ashlike in consistency, don't leave it where it is likely to get bumped, and don't touch it.

As the water in the pan evaporates or is soaked up by the coal, carefully add more.

The more uneven the surface of the coal, the better. A smoothly rounded briquet will not produce as striking a garden as a piece of coal with uneven angles.

Adding a drop of food coloring to the bluing-and-salt dribble mix will produce colored growths. Preparing two or three different colors of dribble mix and "planting" them all in your garden will produce an enchanting rainbow of magic spires.

Button Buzz Saw

MATERIALS NEEDED: *Large button (at least one inch in diameter, and the bigger the better), thin string or thread or dental floss*

THIS SIMPLE AMUSEMENT may be as old as the button itself. You will need one large button, the ordinary type with holes in it, not the type with a loop underneath.

Procedure: Thread a two-foot-long piece of thread, thin string, or dental floss in one of the holes and out again through the hole farthest away from it (in the case of a four-hole button). Dental floss is your best option since it's unusually sturdy. Now tie the ends of the floss together. (Since this is a toy for smaller children, parental assistance may be needed when it comes to tying the knot.)

Hook your index fingers through the loops of the thread, keeping the button somewhere in the middle, and then spin or twirl the button, winding up the string. The buzz saw is ready to go when the string has been crimped into fairly tight coils and your hands are only five or six inches apart.

As you exert pressure, pulling your hands apart, the string will begin to unwind, and the button will twirl rapidly. Just before your hands are the maximum distance apart, relax the pulling pressure. The button has been spinning rapidly as the string untwists, and its momentum will now wind or twist the string in the opposite direction. Let your hands naturally draw closer together again as the string tightens up. Then the button stops, reverses itself, and the procedure is repeated.

Just working the button back and forth, getting the feel of the tension-relaxation rhythm of the string, is by itself a satisfying pastime, but there can be more to it than that.

Once you have pretty good control of the buzz saw (and it's easier to learn than a yo-yo), that control can be put to use. When the rapidly rotating button is brought into contact with a piece of cardboard or newspaper sticking over the edge of a table, the result is a variety of satisfying noises. Still other, different noises can be produced by spinning the buzz saw against other surfaces, such as the edge of a cardboard box, a crumpled wad of newspaper, the rim of a drinking glass, and the top of a wastebasket. But don't be limited by just that list. Within reasonable limits, you can experiment with lots of different surfaces to see what different noises are produced by contact with the spinning-button buzz saw.

Small, lightweight plastic figures (such as toy cowboys) can be set up for the sole purpose of being knocked down by the buzz saw. (If two kids are playing at this together, one can set a jack spinning and the other can try to knock it askew with the buzz saw.) A satisfying mess can be made, if you're willing to clean up afterward, by skimming the spinning button over the surface of a mixing bowl full of water, or passing it through a small heap of flour. (Kids love making messes, and if it's sanctioned by a parent, so much the better. But if the child isn't old enough or reliable enough to clean up after himself or herself, and the parent isn't in the mood to do it, skip the messy activities, and the child can still have a great time being noisy or just watching the thing spin endlessly.)

Up and Around

MATERIALS NEEDED: *Two-foot-long stick, string,* rubber ball*

THIS IS A game for two players. Tie the rubber ball to the center of the stick. A broomstick cut short works well.

The players support the stick by their waists, not using their hands, and sway their bodies so that the ball swings over the stick. This is not a competitive game; there is no one winner. If the players succeed, both of them win. In fact, not only is it not a competitive game, it teaches teamwork and cooperation.

Once the kids get good at swinging the ball over the

---

*The string should be just long enough that, after it is tied around the ball and the stick, the ball just clears the floor. Actual length in inches will vary according to the height of the players. For less experienced or proficient players, the string can be made shorter so less skill and effort are required to get the ball over the stick.

stick, they can work on swinging it around and around till the string is totally wound around the stick. Then, swinging it in the opposite direction, they can unwind it again.

Giant Soap Bubbles

MATERIALS NEEDED: *½ cup liquid dishwashing detergent, 2 tablespoons glycerine, 5 cups cold water, wire coat hanger(s), frying pan (or other large, flat, shallow container), covered plastic container for storing leftover solution*

THESE GIANT BUBBLES are so much fun you'll find yourself joining in with your kids. The fun begins as you mix up the solution: Mix the detergent, glycerine, and water together in the frying pan or similar container. Now bend the coat hangers into circles. If you want to get fancy, you can experiment with triangles or other shapes instead.

Dip the bent coat hangers into the solution and get ready to fill the air with bubbles. Since your coathanger bubble wands are large, waving them in the air is a better method for releasing the bubbles than blowing into them.

To get a whole gang of kids (and parents) involved, mix up several batches of solution and pour it all into a wading pool, then invite the neighbors, or a bunch of your kids' friends, to your house for a bubble festival.

Store the leftover solution in the covered plastic container for another day's fun.

Lollipop Ghosts

MATERIALS NEEDED: *Lollipops with large, round tops (as opposed to the flat kind), white paper napkins, string or yarn, black marker*

THIS PASTIME IS simplicity personified, and parental help won't be needed unless the child is too young to use the marker respectfully or tie a knot.

Procedure: For each ghost, open a paper napkin and drape it over a lollipop, then tie the napkin securely under the bulb of the lollipop with the string. With the marker, draw two eyes. (Elongated eyes are better for a more ghostly appearance.)

Now you have homemade ghosts, and what you do with them is entirely up to your imagination. The most usual uses are as dolls or as puppets, holding the ghosts by the lollipop sticks and manipulating them that way.

Thread-Spool Puppets

MATERIALS NEEDED: Empty spool of thread, paint or marking pens, paste or glue, yarn or crepe paper or cotton. Optional: Cloth or construction paper

YOUR CHILD CAN put on puppet shows with old-fashioned homemade thread-spool puppets. Half the fun is in giving the show; half the fun is in actually making the puppets. The more kids involved, the larger the cast of puppets can be, but one child can put on a fine show by himself or herself.

Save your old, empty spools of thread. When you have several, the kids can start making puppets.

Procedure: Draw the puppet's face with paint or thin-line marking pens. Make the hair out of yarn or use cut-up crepe paper, in either case glued on, or paste cotton on top of the spool for a white-haired appearance.

Sharpen a pencil. (The parent can then break off the lead point for extra safety if s/he wishes, but an unsharpened pencil will be too thick to fit in the spool.) Glue the sharpened end of the pencil and insert it in the spool.

You now have a rudimentary puppet. (An older and/or more creative child can add clothing. Clothing can be made from material, of course, but the simplest way to make the puppet's clothes is to cut one-dimensional clothing out of construction paper and glue that to the front of the pencil, allowing enough room at the bottom to grip the pencil.)

Now you have heads with faces and hair, and possibly clothing as well. The puppets are ready. You can improvise, just allowing one puppet to talk to the audience, or two or more puppets to talk to each other. If you're particularly ambitious or creative, you can write a script and put on a complete show that tells a story, or act out an old familiar fairy tale.

Educational Activities

Homemade Alphabet Book

MATERIALS NEEDED: Magazines and newspapers, as well as any other media suitable for cutting up, such as old greeting cards, photos that didn't come out quite right, etc., scissors, paste or glue, construction paper or cardboard

MAKING A HOMEMADE alphabet book is a good activity for young kids that combines arts-and-crafts fun with educational value. The child cuts out a large-print example of each letter of the alphabet from a magazine or newspaper. (Newsprint is, of course, messier to work with, and letters from a magazine, especially a magazine ad, are more likely to be in color, a plus for making the book bright and cheery.)

Each letter gets pasted on a piece of cardboard or construction paper. Then the child looks for pictures of objects that begin with that letter, and pastes these pictures on the same cardboard or paper. For some letters, such as *X*, your child may have to hunt long and hard just for one picture of a xylophone. If s/he starts getting frustrated, allow him or her to draw a picture if s/he's so inclined. For other letters, there may be so many pictures available (if you have a large supply of magazines) that s/he may choose to overlap pictures collage-style.

Encourage your child to think creatively. Consider parts of a picture as well as the picture as a whole. For instance, if you're looking at a picture of a person, what letter of the alphabet do you think that picture represents? Actually it could be *P* for *person*, *W* or *M* for *woman* or *man*, *D* for *driver* if they're seated in a car, etc. Cutting out just the face or head in the picture gives the child *F* or *H*, and cutting out the individual features will give *E* (*eyes, eyebrows, ears*), *N* (*nose*), *M* (*mouth*), *H* (*hair*), *L* (*lips*), and possibly *T* (*teeth*). Moving down the body, your child can find *H* (*hands*), *A* (*arms*), *B* (*body*), *L* (*legs*), *F* (*feet*), and so on. The same is true of a picture of a house *(W: windows, D: door,* etc.), of a dog (*C: collar, T: tail, P: paws,* etc.), and of many other things as well, in which the whole is the sum of many parts.

This is an activity that won't be accomplished in one sitting. Encourage your child to spend as long at a clip as s/he has patience for, putting the project away unfinished to be returned to another day. With twenty-six letters of the alphabet, and multiple pictures to illustrate each, the alphabet book will answer the question, "Mommy, what can I do now?" on an awful lot of occasions.

The Winning Ticket

MATERIALS NEEDED: *Two cut-out squares of construction paper in each of as many different colors as you can get, two baskets or boxes or mixing bowls*

THIS IS A game with educational value for small children. Besides teaching them colors, it teaches concentration. It's a game for you, the parent, to play with one or more kids at a time.

One ticket (square of construction paper) of each

color is placed in each basket or bowl, and then one of the bowls is placed across the room from you and your child. From the other bowl, in front of you, you draw a ticket and show it to your child. Now, without that ticket in his/her hand, the child goes across the room to the other bowl and hunts for the matching ticket, remembering what color s/he's looking for. If the child is in the process of learning the names of the colors, you can require that s/he name it as well as retrieve it.

The mental activity in this game requires that the child hold the specified color in his/her mind while crossing the room, and that s/he be able to sort through the various colored tickets in the basket to find the right one from memory.

Spools of thread, crayons, or other items that you can match up in pairs of identical colors may be substituted for the construction-paper tickets.

Variation: For the child learning his or her alphabet, substitute tickets of the same color but with letters written on them. Have one *A* in each bowl, one *B*, and so forth. If you think your child can't sort through twenty-six letters and find the right one, use only part of the alphabet at a time.

Variation: For children who have learned their capital letters but are now learning the lowercase letters, write the capitals on the tickets in one bowl, and the lowercase versions on the tickets in the other bowl. Then, if you show the child a capital *E*, for instance, s/he has to go to the other bowl and find a lowercase *e*.

Nonverbal Communication

MATERIALS NEEDED: *None*

YOU OR YOUR child make nonsense sounds, as if carrying on a conversation, and the other person responds with facial expressions or body movements showing how the sound made the listener feel. A "conversation" develops, a conversation without words, just nonsense syllables, sounds, facial expressions, and body movements.

A wide range of emotions can be covered in this conversation, and conveyed from one partner to the other. The child should take away from this seemingly silly game some understanding of how inflection or tone affect whatever words we say, often in not-so-subtle ways, as well as how facial expressions and body language can convey thoughts and feelings too.

Hug a Tree

MATERIALS NEEDED: *Trees, blindfold*

BLINDFOLD YOUR CHILD in an area with a number of trees, and lead him or her to one tree by a circuitous route, so s/he doesn't know which tree s/he's standing in front of. Now instruct the child to explore the tree using his or her hands. S/he may smell the tree carefully too if s/he wishes. Then lead your child back to the starting point by a circuitous route, so it won't be easy to find the tree just by retracing steps.

Remove the blindfold and have him or her try to find the same tree again by remembering the way it felt, possibly the way it smelled, and anything else familiar about it, such as a particular unevenness of the ground around it or other discernible characteristics.

Letter of the Day Game

MATERIALS NEEDED: *Paper, pencil or crayon*

THIS GAME IS a fun way to help lay the groundwork for reading. It teaches children to recognize the different letters of the alphabet, and you'll be surprised at how quickly even little ones catch on. After all, if a child is old enough to recognize and distinguish from one another the faces of family members, or to know the difference between a Tootsie Roll and a can of spinach, it's not so surprising that s/he can begin to recognize a few letters as well. Perhaps little ones will have trouble differentiating between *M* and *N* and *W*, or between *O* and *C* and *G*, or between *U* and *V*, at least at first, but some letters are more easily discernible than others, and even slow progress is still progress. Eventually, s/he'll learn them all, and this game makes the learning fun.

Every morning, choose a specific letter of the alphabet. Start with more distinctive ones like *A* or *Y* or *T*. Print the letter in a large block capital while the child watches. Then, as you go about the day's routine, make a game of pointing that letter out every time you see it.

If you and the child go to the store, you may see today's special letter on signs in the supermarket or in shop windows, on labels on foods, or on boxes. Watch for traffic signs. If the supermarket cashier, the baker clerk, or other people you encounter are wearing name tags, check them for the letter in question. Watch gas station signs. Look at billboards.

Have your child join in the search and praise him or her lavishly if s/he finds the letter. You can guide or give hints: "Do you see today's special letter on this cash register receipt?" "What do you see on that chewing gum pack?"

At home, look at the big lettering in newspaper or magazine ads. What about brand names written on your stove, fridge, washer, dryer? Your car? The calendar on the wall? Letters are all around us.

Your child may find it easier to recognize the letters if you can personify them—for example, a capital *T* looks like it has arms held straight out to the side; a capital *C* looks like a person curled up on the floor.

At the end of the day, talk briefly about all the places you saw today's special letter, print it again, ask your child if s/he remembers its name, and perhaps even ask him or her to try printing it himself/herself. Praise his or her efforts, even if s/he needs more than a little help and is still off the mark when s/he prints it.

The next day: another letter.

As your child gets older and starts learning the lowercase letters, have him or her look for those in addition to the capitals.

And when s/he is beginning to learn to spell, vary the game by having him or her look for objects that begin with the letter of the day. Again, you can guide and give hints. If you decide that today's letter is *B,* ask, "What am I wearing that starts with *B?*" (Blouse.)

"And what's on my blouse that starts with *B?*" (Button.) Soon the child will be pointing out bread and bananas triumphantly. Always be sure to give praise for a right answer, even if coaching was involved.

How Do You Feel?

MATERIALS NEEDED: *Paper and pencil*

LIST VARIOUS EMOTIONS on a piece of paper, leaving plenty of space next to each emotion. Then have your child draw a face illustrating each of these emotions. Some of the emotions you list might be happy, sad, confident, bashful, angry, bored, disappointed, ecstatic, disgusted, etc. If your child is too young to read some of the names of the emotions, read them aloud.

To give your child an example of what you're looking for, you may wish to draw the traditional happy face next to the word *happy*.

This exercise will help children recognize the different emotions and be more cognizant of what they're feeling at different times. Of course, your child will think s/he's just having fun drawing.

Homemade Sun Dial

MATERIALS NEEDED: *Stiff cardboard, scissors, compass, crayons, glue or paste, penknife (to be used by a parent)*

THIS IS DEFINITELY a project for parent and child to work on together, as it involves not only sharp scissors, unsuitable for younger children, but also a penknife, which an adult should certainly be the one to use.

Procedure: Cut a six-inch square from the cardboard. Using the compass, draw the largest circle that will fit on the square, then draw a circle one-half inch inside the first circle. Mark off the edge of the outer circle in twelve equal spaces, and write the numbers of the hours, one through twelve, between the inner and outer circles.

The parent should now use the penknife to cut a slot in the upper half of the dial's face, beginning at the exact center and continuing straight to the inner circle just under the 12 at the top. Cut clear through the cardboard, and make it as wide as the thickness of the cardboard.

Then cut a piece of cardboard into a triangle, making two of the sides the exact same length as the slot you've cut in the dial's face. Split one edge of that triangle in half, up one-quarter inch, carefully separating the cardboard in the center. Then slip that edge through the slot in the sun dial's face, making sure the triangle slants upward from the center so the peak is at the twelve. Glue the tops of the split edges and press them to the back of the dial to secure them.

Place the finished sun dial outdoors on a flat surface, in a spot that receives sun all day. Place it with the back, elevated edge of the triangle (twelve o'clock) pointed due north. The sun will cause the triangle to cast a shadow on the sun dial. If the shadow falls on the two, it is two o'clock. As the sun moves across the sky, the shadow will move around the numbers of the sun dial.

As cardboard is not impermeable to rain, you may want to bring the sun dial indoors during inclement weather, when it will not function anyhow, of course!

Weather Chart

MATERIALS NEEDED: *Large piece of poster board or cardboard, marker, small weather symbols (sun, clouds, rain, snow, lightning) cut from newspapers or magazines, tape*

ON THE POSTER board, the parent makes the appropriate number of squares for a monthly calendar. (If the child is old enough, s/he may be able to do this himself or herself.) Number each box with the appropriate date. Be sure your squares are large enough to hold the weather symbols you have clipped.

Each day, the child tapes the appropriate symbol(s) onto the correct day on the calendar for that day's weather. For example, if it is cloudy on the twenty-third, the child would tape a cloud on the square marked "23." If it's sunny in the morning with thunderstorms in the afternoon on the twenty-fourth, the child would tape a sun and a lightning bolt on the square marked "24."

Global Dressing

MATERIALS NEEDED: A globe, small pictures of clothing clipped from newspapers or magazines, tape

THE PARENT PREPARES this activity by clipping small pictures of various types of clothing from publications, assembling a wide variety, ranging from shorts, swimsuits, and T-shirts to winter coats, snow boots, and mufflers.

The parent explains how weather and temperatures vary in relation to a place's location on the globe, its nearness to the equator or the poles. Then, naming a country, the parent helps the child find that country on the globe, and, based on the knowledge of how temperatures vary by distance from the equator or poles, asks the child how people in that specific country might dress. The child then tapes an appropriate article of clothing on that country on the globe.

Conflict Resolution

MATERIALS NEEDED: *Index cards on which the parent has written various conflicts*

CONFLICTS CANNOT BE avoided, but children who have learned the appropriate way to deal with conflicts can keep them from escalating. On index cards, write such conflict situations as: "My friend copies off my paper at school and I get caught"; "Somebody goes through my private things"; "Somebody tries to talk me into doing something I don't want to do"; "My friends call me too late and my mom gets mad at me"; "Somebody at school says I look ugly"; "Somebody is telling lies about me"; or "Nobody believes me when I'm telling the truth." These suggestions are, of course, just that: suggestions. Feel free to use them, change them, or discard them completely in favor of other conflicts you feel are more likely to occur in your child's life.

For each index card, have the child first state how that particular conflict would make him or her feel. Then have him or her reason out an appropriate response. Point out various pitfalls to the child if his/her responses are not the best. For instance, if the child's response is, "I'd punch him in the nose," ask the child what the consequences of that action are likely to be, and whether that action is likely to bring the conflict to a peaceful resolution or if it would, in fact, escalate the conflict.

After the child has framed what s/he believes is an

appropriate response for all the conflicts you have listed on the index cards, and those responses have been analyzed by the two of you, have the child come up with some conflicts of his or her own. These may be situations that have occurred to his or her friends, or just situations that s/he imagines might come up at some time. They may, however, be real situations that have already occurred in his or her life, or that s/he is facing currently, and you can help him or her solve these conflicts by talking him or her through the resolution.

Lacing Board/Sewing Card

MATERIALS NEEDED: *Pieces of pegboard, marker, shoelaces or yarn (if yarn is used, masking tape or duct tape will also be needed)*

YOU CAN PREPARE as many of these as you wish ahead of time, then turn your child loose with them and let him or her have a great time by himself/herself.

For permanent lacing boards, cut pieces of pegboard (the kind used to hang tools in a shop) into rectangles, perhaps ten inches by fourteen inches. Decide what shapes or pictures will go on each board. They should be simple, easily recognizable items such as fish, sailboats, jack o'lanterns, daisies, hands, and birds.

With a marker, draw in portions of the outlines of the pictures, leaving it for your child to fill in the rest of the outlines using the yarn or shoelaces. The combination of marker lines and yarn will produce a picture the child can take credit for creating.

Depending on the age of your child, you may have to show her or him how to always start from the underside of the board, how to sew the yarn back through the board where the black marker line starts, how to bring the yarn back up at the other line, and so on.

Either you or your child ties a fat knot at the ends of the various pieces of yarn or shoelaces, and then your child begins lacing the picture. If yarn is used rather than shoelaces, your or your child will need to make the front of each strand stiff enough to thread it easily through the holes. This is accomplished by a tight wrap of masking tape or duct tape.

Lacing cards can also be made from tagboard, cardboard, or old file folders. They are less durable than pegboard but have the advantage that you can punch the holes wherever you like, using a hole puncher. If you use a big piece of cardboard, and the hole puncher won't reach the middle, you can punch out the holes by pushing a pencil all the way through and then trimming off the ragged edges. If you wish, you can use round reinforcements to keep the holes from tearing out.

Variation: Cut pictures from magazines and paste them onto pieces of cardboard, then punch holes at intervals around the picture. Your child goes around the holes twice. The first time the yarn shows above the card from A to B, from C to D, from E to F, and so on; the second time s/he covers the blank spaces from B to C, from D to E, and so on.

Variation: The child can use unmarked pegboard to create his or her own designs, not necessarily pictures, by running various colors of yarn from hole to hole in patterns that catch his or her fancy.

You and I

MATERIALS NEEDED: Poster board and marker or paper and pencil

HAVE YOUR CHILD generate some accusatory statements. Write them down on the poster board or paper. If the child needs examples to get started, possibilities are "You never do your homework"; "You act like such a baby"; or "You never listen to me."

When you have compiled a list, ask your child how s/he feels when hearing such accusatory statements. Note the continual occurrence of the word "you" in these statements.

Now have your child rephrase each accusatory statement, taking out the word "you" and substituting the word "I," so that rather than "You never listen to me," the statement would be "I'm afraid that I won't be able to say what I want to say to you when I'm interrupted."

When all the accusatory statements have been recast in such a manner, ask your child how s/he feels hearing the recast statements. A calm and meaningful, productive discussion should ensue.

Making Choices

MATERIALS NEEDED: *A newspaper*

THIS IS AN exercise in ethics and values. Read your child a crime story from the local newspaper. Perhaps the story is of an armed robbery. First ask your child what the story was about, and have him or her tell you, in his/her own words, the story you just read to him or her. Make sure s/he understands it.

Now ask the child why s/he thinks the person might have committed the crime. Could the robber just hate other people? Might he have been out of work with a family to feed? What else might make a person do such a thing? Was it the right thing to do? Why or why not? What could they have done instead of committing the robbery? Did the person or store that was robbed do anything to deserve being robbed? Was it fair? (Kids have a great interest in what's fair or unfair.) Does your child think the robber is a happy person? Might he be a frightened or angry person? How could he become happier?

These questions involve numerous assumptions, and of course the child's guesses may be off the mark of reality in the situation, but the point is to get the child involved in analyzing ethics and choices.

Describing Pairs

MATERIALS NEEDED: *Identical pairs of pictures cut from magazines, newspapers, or other sources, pasted on cardboard*

THIS COOPERATIVE, NONCOMPETITIVE game for two small children helps develop language and communications skills. You need to prepare for it by cutting out the pictures ahead of time, possibly buying two copies of the same magazine or newspaper in order to get matching pictures. There should be some similarity between the pictures. You don't want one pair of pictures of a car, one pair of pictures of a house, one pair of pictures of a bike. Rather, it's better if they're all pictures of something somewhat similar: people are best, houses or buildings are another possibility.

Choose several pairs of pictures from among the ones you've cut and pasted, and place them facedown between the two kids. Each child draws one picture and holds it so the other cannot see. Then one child describes his or her picture to the other, without letting the other child see it. The other child can ask as many questions as s/he wants.

If they decide they have a pair, they place them faceup on the table. If they're right, and the pictures match, they lay them aside and each picks another picture, repeating the process, but this time it is the other child's turn to do the describing. If they are wrong, and the pictures are not a pair, they are placed back on the table facedown, and the game proceeds.

How Observant Are You?

MATERIALS NEEDED: *None*

HAVE YOUR CHILD study your physical appearance for thirty seconds, noting such things as clothing, accessories, etc. Then leave the room and change five things about your appearance. For example, unbutton a collar button, roll your shirt sleeves up, change a ring from one hand to another, change shoes, change your headband (women) or tie (men).

Now return to the room where your child is and see if s/he can identify the five things you've changed.

Your child may want a turn at trying to fool you and test your powers of observation next.

Miss Miller Likes

MATERIALS NEEDED: *Paper and pencil*

THIS GAME FOR children old enough to read tests their powers of observation. The object is for them to discover what the particular quality is that differentiates what Miss Miller likes from what Miss Miller doesn't like.

Educational Activities

Write the following down for your child in advance:

Miss Miller likes:	*But not:*
kittens	cats
puppies	dogs
boots	shoes
walls	ceilings
cooking	eating
running	hiking
pizza	hamburgers
sleeping	waking

Your child can take as long as s/he wants to study the lists and try to discern what it is that differentiates the one list from the other. If you wish, you may give hints at your discretion.

If your child is observant, s/he may eventually realize that Miss Miller likes words with double letters, like in her name.

Car Games

I'm Going Shopping

MATERIALS NEEDED: **None**

THIS GAME, WHILE it can be played anywhere, is very suitable for keeping kids occupied during a car ride. It can be played by two or more people, which can include parents but doesn't have to. It's a memory game, the object being to remember an ever-growing list of objects in alphabetical order. Each time a player fails to remember an object, or remembers a wrong object, s/he is out of the game. The winner is the last player left after the others have been eliminated.

The first player leads off with, "I'm going shopping and I'm buying———" and finishes with an object starting with *A*, perhaps apples. The next player repeats the first player's shopping list and adds an item of his/her own, beginning with the next letter of the alphabet: "I'm going shopping and I'm buying apples and bananas." The third player might say, "I'm going shopping and I'm buying apples, bananas, and coffee." And so on.

The items on the shopping list don't have to be grocery story items. In fact, they don't have to be sensible. The shopping list could start with aardvarks, bristles, and color TVs.

Variation: The shopping list is made up of brand names only: "I'm going shopping and I'm buying Alpha Bits, Brillo, Cheerios, Dunkin' Donuts—"

Don't worry about what the kids will come up with for *X*. It's unlikely that any group of kids will ever get anywhere near that far.

Alphabet on Wheels

MATERIALS NEEDED: *None*

THIS GAME HAS two things going for it: Like any car game, it helps keep kids occupied while traveling and fighting the fidgets, and it also helps them brush up on their alphabet or spelling skills. There are two ways to play.

On a more basic level, alphabet skills, the idea is to look for each letter of the alphabet in turn. First the kids (or just one child—this works with just one as it need not be a competitive game and there is no winner) look for a word with the letter *A* in it. They can check billboards, speed signs, highway exit signs, or street signs, even license plates of other cars—with letters on it. Only when an *A* has been found do the kids start looking for *B*, then *C*, etc.

With more than one child in the car, a certain element of competitiveness enters into the game because each child will want to be the first one to spot each letter of the alphabet. But as there's no actual winner or scoring, this game is just as suitable for one child as for six.

If you're driving down Main Street or on a highway filled with billboards where signs abound, and the game is getting too easy, you can make it a requirement that the letter the kids are searching for has to be at the beginning of a word, not just anywhere in a word. Now they're looking for a word beginning with *A*, a word beginning with *B*, and so forth.

For older kids who are beyond simple alphabet games

and into spelling games, instead of looking for words along the road, they can look for objects beginning with certain letters. If you're driving through the streets of town, apples in front of a fruit market could provide *A*. On a highway, a billboard could be *B*. The curb could be *C*, as could clouds overhead, and a dog you pass could be *D*.

Admittedly, this variation is harder, but that makes it more interesting for the older children, as well as making them think harder and brush up on their spelling skills. As an added fillip for even older kids, you can require them to spell the object correctly before taking credit for that letter of the alphabet and starting to look for the next one.

If the scenery in the area in which you're driving doesn't provide a whole lot of opportunities for finding objects, broaden the scope to include objects and people in the car. *A* could be an arm, *B* could be anyone's body, *C* could be the clock on the dashboard, and *D* the dashboard itself. Multiple uses of the same object are permitted: The striping painted on the road can be *L* for *line* (or for *lane divider*), *S* for *stripe*, and *P* for *paint*. It can also be *W* for *white* or *Y* for *yellow*, according to which color it is. The road itself can serve for *R (road)*, *S (street)*, *H (highway)*, *P (pavement)* and even *C* or *A* or *M (concrete* or *asphalt* or *macadam)*.

Geographical License Plate Games

MATERIALS NEEDED: *None, or possibly pad and pencil or map of the United States*

Basic play: The child keeps track of all the different

states represented by license plates encountered along the road. With either a map or an alphabetical list of states in front of him/her, s/he marks off each state as s/he spots a license plate from that state.

Note: If a map is used, rather than just a list of states, the child will gain practice in learning geography, and where the states are actually located.

Variation: To make the states more interesting for the child, you can offer premiums for difficult accomplishments. If you're driving on the East Coast, offer a prize for spotting something unlikely such as an Oregon plate. If you're not into making it quite that difficult, offer a prize for spotting all the states east of the Mississippi. Prizes can be a bunch of grapes, a candy bar, a stop for ice cream, a dime for every state west of the Rockies, or whatever suits you.

Variation: Older children can be offered points in the game, or rewards, if they can name the capital of the state whose plate they've spotted. If you're knowledgeable about the states yourself, spotting a plate can be a springboard to a discussion about the state's major products or crops, and anything else you can tell the kids about that state, which will give them a leg up in school. If your kids are sports fans, you can even include a discussion of major professional and college sports teams from that state.

If you do have an atlas or map in the car with you, you can examine it with the kids and discuss the states whose plates they've spotted, and the route these travelers might have taken to get to where you spotted them. (Over the Rockies? Across the Mississippi? Along the shore? Through which other states?) This will give the kids a better feel for geography, and a more cohesive feel for what states border on what other states and what mountains or rivers figure prominently in what states. Then the state is more than just an abstract name to the kids. If you're up on history, you can also get into a discussion with the kids about what significant historical events have taken place in that state over the course of the nation's history.

Variation: You can even quiz the kids about the states whose plates they spot, awarding points only if they can answer a question about that state, which can vary in toughness according to the age of your kids: "Name two states that border on Alabama." "What are the principal products of Michigan?" "Is Arizona mainly arable land or desert?"

The simple metal rectangle whose official purpose is merely to prove that a vehicle tax has been paid can prove the source of a good deal of time-consuming fun—and education—on a car trip.

Progressive Stories

MATERIALS NEEDED: *None*

ALTHOUGH THIS ACTIVITY can be a wonderful pastime anytime, from a camping trip to a rainy Saturday, it's particularly well suited to car trips. Any number can play, and in fact it gets wilder and more fun the more people are involved.

One person starts telling a story. You, the parent, may want to lead it off yourself, whether or not you continue playing along with the kids after that. (Of course, if you have only one child in the car with you, you'll definitely be needed to keep playing along, but the game is fun, and you might find yourself hooked, even if you're not needed.)

Any story will do, any situation, any characters, real or fictional, of your own invention or someone else's.

Grandma, your son's friend Bobby, a well-known cartoon character, a historical character, or someone you just now made up out of the blue: "Once there was a boy named Dennis, who lived by the ocean and had a pet turtle named Blabble. One morning Dennis decided to ride his bike over to his best friend's house. Dennis zoomed down the street toward Chris's house, and as he went around the corner onto Maple Street, he saw—"

At any distance into the narrative, from a couple of sentences to several minutes of scene setting, the storyteller breaks off the narrative and turns the story over to the next person. As the story grows, an astonishing array of details and circumstances get packed into the tale—and it's always likely that the scene will shift to Brazil or Jupiter or a secret passageway in the Bensons' house.

This activity develops and encourages creativity, originality, and a hang-loose sense of playfulness. If a story loses the participants' interest, it's easy to turn it around in another direction. If it's truly played out, and there are no interesting avenues left to explore, start another story.

These tales tend to become cliffhangers. Storytellers often try to lead the characters into improbable or difficult situations, then stop the story and turn it over to the next player, sticking him or her with the difficult task of getting Our Hero (or Heroine) out of the jam s/he's in. Or the storytellers spin wilder and ever more imaginative yarns, each one trying to outdo all previous narrators with his or her inventiveness.

A parent who wants to foster even greater originality in her or his kids can ban storybook characters, TV characters, and the like from these stories, insisting on all original characters. But sometimes, especially for self-conscious kids, those unsure of their creativity, and those playing the game for the first time, it's easier if they don't feel constrained to make up the situation *and* the characters. And so, while you might not choose to outright suggest that they make up a story about the Ninja Turtles or Mickey Mouse, you could allow it if they did.

Once the kids have played this game one time, they may not even need you to start the game off at all, especially if at least one of your kids has a particularly fertile imagination.

Tall Tale Contest

MATERIALS NEEDED: *None*

ANOTHER CAR GAME involving vivid imaginations and nothing else is the tall tale contest. This is particularly well suited for a car trip with a parent and one child, though it works just fine with other combinations, too. It isn't really a competition in the sense of there being a winner, though generally when you're telling tall tales, each tale-spinner tries to top the tales that were told before. The tall tale contest has an honorable place in the history of the American West.

If the child isn't familiar with the concept of tall tales, you, the parent, will wish to start things off, spinning a whopper that's somewhere between implausible and impossible. The sillier or more improbable it is, the better the child will get the idea. People can suddenly disappear off the face of the earth, only to have it ultimately revealed that they are being reeled up by fishermen on another planet. Or you can tell about a man so big he used the whole lawn to wipe his feet and plucked an apple tree out of the ground to brush the flies off him. When he was thirsty, he drank a tanker truck full of milk. The story can be as impossible to believe as you can make it. There's no limit. None.

There are many benefits a child can derive from playing this game, beyond the fact that it passes time during a car trip (or a wait in the doctor's office, or in line in the supermarket, or just on a rainy day at home). Obviously, the child's imagination is developed. His/her creativity is challenged. S/he's encouraged to develop ideas: S/he's encouraged to think. Since the tales are told in turns, s/he practices taking turns and waiting patiently and politely for his/her turn.

Originality should be strongly encouraged. This is definitely an exercise in creativity, and the child should be prompted or led into making up his/her own characters, rather than telling stories about cartoon, movie, TV, or book characters. The adaptation of such characters by the child can be expressly forbidden by the rules, deflected by suggestion, or simply extinguished by parental example. You can guide the child into an understanding of the wonderful richness of originality and the poverty of imitation. Who knows—you may discover you have a budding Nobel literature prizewinner in your family! But you're out for fun; don't turn the game into a literary lesson on story structure. The idea is just to stretch the imagination.

The swapping of tall tales can go on for miles, depending on the number of people involved, the age of the child or children, and the depth of their imaginations. The delight grows as the child grasps the idea of how to construct a tall tale, begins to hit his or her stride, and devises wilder and wilder outrageous tales.

These sessions can also be an occasion to introduce your child to some classic stories from the rich tradition of American tall tales. When you get home from your car trip, or at the next available opportunity, stop in at the library and borrow a book or two about Mike Fink or Pecos Bill, and introduce your child to the classic tales. It may even get him or her away from the TV for a night or two—or turn him or her into a devoted reader.

I'm Thinking of a Color

MATERIALS NEEDED: *None*

ONE PERSON STARTS by picking an object in the car—say, the needle on the speedometer. "I'm thinking of something red," that person says, and the next player in turn gets to ask one yes-or-no question to help identify it. "Is it on Dad's side of the car?" or "Is it in the front of the car?" or "Is someone wearing it?" The first person who guesses correctly wins, and gets to pick the object to be guessed next turn. A player who guesses an object but guesses wrong is out of the game till next turn.

The Street Sign Name Game

MATERIALS NEEDED: *None*

DEPENDING WHETHER YOU'RE driving in town or on the interstate, you can use street signs, billboards, or exit signs for this. The object is for each player to find all the letters in his/her name as you pass various signs along the way. Whether you ask the players to find all the letters in just their first names, or first and middle and last, will depend on their names, their ages, their ability to spell and to recognize letters, and the number and type of signs you're likely to be passing along the way.

If they all find their names quickly but haven't tired of the game, have them look to spell friends' names, storybook characters' names, even names of their favorite foods, the colors of the rainbow, ice cream flavors, or whatever interests them.

Memory and Knowledge Games

MATERIALS NEEDED: *Paper and pencil*

THIS ONE IS almost like a pop quiz on wheels, but present it as a game and the kids may not realize they're being tested and educated. The questions can be far-ranging, and of your discretion, but the most common ones are geographical: "Name the seven continents." "Name the fifty states." "Name the fifty state capitols." "Name all the oceans in the world."

You can give each child a different question to answer, in turn, or you can have all the kids chime in at once with as many answers as they can come up with. You can award points for correct answers, if you want to build rewards into the game, but it isn't necessary; meeting the challenge is usually sufficient incentive for the kids to put on their thinking caps.

For smaller kids, you can ask easier questions: "How many streets can you name between our house and Tommy's house?"

If only one parent is in the car, driving, s/he will not be able to write down the answers as they're shouted out, in which case one of the kids will have to assume that chore.

Imagination Stretches

MATERIALS NEEDED: *None*

THIS CAN DETERIORATE into a silly-session, but if the kids get a fit of the giggles, who cares? It sure beats the bored blahs and the perpetual whine of "Are we there yet?"

The premise is simple: You, the parent, come up with a question such as, "How many uses can you think of for a hat?" The kids have to be creative with their answers, but by no means do they have to be sensible. Possible answers to the hat challenge are: "To water a horse." "To plant flowers in." "To hold thread." "To use as a target for a coin toss."

They may even come up with answers like that last one that become the premise of a new game for them to play when you get home.

There are no winners or losers in this game, just a group of involved kids who are beating boredom while exercising their creativity. Well—maybe there are winners: you, the parents, who don't have to listen to "How much longer?" while the kids are having fun playing the game.

Arts & Crafts Projects

Custom Stationery

MATERIALS NEEDED: *Typing paper or construction paper, crayons or markers*

THIS ACTIVITY IS more popular with girls than boys, but there's no reason for boys not to engage in it, too, if they want.

Procedure: Decorate sheets of typing paper with whatever designs appeal to you—curlicues, lacework, a plain line border—and personalize it with your name, or "From the desk of Chris." You can make all the sheets try to look as uniform as possible, or you can even try different designs on different sheets.

Now you have your own special, personalized stationery on which to write thank-you notes, letters to friends, and those all-important notes to Grandma. You can even make a set of stationery for Grandma as a gift, perhaps wrapping it in homemade wrapping paper (see page 29) and tying the package up in a pretty ribbon.

Vegetable Prints

MATERIALS NEEDED: *Tempera paint, paper towels, paring knife, paper, assorted vegetables such as carrot, celery, broccoli, potato, parsley*

THIS ACTIVITY WILL adapt itself easily to the increasing artistic skill and sophistication of older children, but is still a thorough (and messy!) delight to younger kids.

The child will be creating variously colored ink pads and making stamps from some of the contents of your refrigerator. With smaller children, parental aid will be very necessary, especially when it comes to using the knife; older kids can do it on their own and may find themselves occupied for hours with this activity, making elaborate artistic productions.

Procedure: Make the ink pad by soaking a piece of paper towel, folded over at least twice, in tempera paint. (The number of colors of ink pads is limited only by parental patience and pocketbook, and the selection available at the local art supply or stationery store.)

A carrot cut in three pieces will yield three different-size circle stamps. Sliced celery gives you a C-shaped stamp. And broccoli and parsley, inked and pressed to the paper, give unpredictable and interesting designs and curlicues. Then, of course, there is the potato. After slicing it in half, the child or parent can use a paring knife, kitchen knife, or pocket knife to carve away parts of the sliced end of the potato, leaving behind a design, an initial, or even a simple picture. Checkerboard designs, wavy lines, circles, or abstract art are all possible.

If the child isn't old enough for knives, s/he can skip the potato, or the parent can do the carving. If the child is doing the cutting, the parent may need to explain the concept that for a letter (other than *A, H, I, M, O, T, U, V, W,* and *X*) to come out printed right-way-around, it needs to be carved in reverse.

The vegetable stamps can be used to make artwork of the hang-on-the-fridge variety, or to decorate homemade wrapping paper (see page 29), or in lieu of crayons or markers in the designing of custom stationery (see previous item).

Vegetable prints offer a bonus that's unusual in the art world: Unused materials (minus the inked portions) can always be eaten by the hungry artist or his or her family!

Colored Paper Doilies

MATERIALS NEEDED: *White paper lace doilies, crayons, paste, small (dessert-size) paper plates*

THIS IS A simple project for a child of any age.
Procedure: Simply color the doily with crayons, paying some attention to the flower and lace patterns and making the color harmonious with the design. Then, when it's finished, paste it on a small paper plate, which can either be colored in matching or contrasting colors or left white to set off the colored doily. You can then hang the finished artwork on your wall, or of course it can always join the rest of the art on the fridge.

Sponge-Printed Greeting Cards

MATERIALS NEEDED: *Sponges (small dishpan size), poster paint, glue, cans, drawing paper, cake pans, marker, scissors*

YOU MAY NEED to help your child with this one, especially the younger kids.

Procedure: Decide on the figure you want to print, and draw the outline of it on a piece of paper. Then cut out the figure. Possibilities include hearts, simple flowers, birds, apples, stars, Christmas trees, or anything simple to cut that is recognizable by its outline. Or cut from a magazine a small picture that you want to print the outline of.

Now take the cut-out figure and place it against the sponge, tracing the outline onto the sponge. Then cut the sponge along these lines and glue the sponge to the bottom of the can. You now have the stamp with which you'll print the cards. Of course you can cut several sponges in several different designs.

To make the card, fold the drawing paper in half so it looks like a greeting card that opens up. The print will go on the outside and the message on the inside.

Place the poster paints in the cake pans. Holding the can, dip the sponge into the paint, then press onto the paper. You can print your one design in several places, in one color or several, or you can print different designs—say a moon and several stars, or a tree and a flower.

You can also use sponge printing to make your own homemade wrapping paper, printing on a roll of butcher paper.

String Paintings

MATERIALS NEEDED: Tempera paint, butcher paper or other paper appropriate for painting, lengths of string from one to two feet long

YOU'LL PROBABLY WANT to put down newspaper or plastic to protect the table the child is going to work on before s/he gets going. This project is suitable for kids of all ages, though the young ones will need your help.

Procedure: Prepare the paper by folding it in half and making a crease. Then open it back up and lay it on the table. Dip a length of string in paint, keeping the held end clean. Hold the string over the paint bowl till it's through dripping.

Lay the string on the paper, lowering it slowly and letting it loop and twist and ooze onto the page. Let the clean end of the string extend off the edge of the paper. Repeat this procedure with as many strings and colors as desired. An overdose of painty strings will result in some smearing of the colors and blurring of the lines; experimentation and experience will be your best guide.

When enough colored strings have been allowed to droop and twine on the paper, fold the paper in half once again, pressing the strings between the two halves of the paper. While you are still pressing the folded-over top sheet firmly, pull each of the strings out by the clean end, from between the pressed-together halves of the paper.

Every string painting is unique, all are intriguing, and many are strikingly attractive.

Scratch Paintings

MATERIALS NEEDED: *Paper (ordinary typing paper will do, but heavier paper is preferable), crayons including black, coin*

Procedure: Cover all of the paper with random stripings and swirls and blocks and swoops of different colors of crayon. There is no need to attempt to form a pattern, draw a picture, or be at all artistic in the way it's laid down. Random coloring is what's called for. Just be sure the entire page is covered with color.

Now take the black crayon and cover every inch of color you've just applied. When the paper is totally black, like a picture of a crow at midnight, use the edge of a coin to lightly scratch lines and swirls through the black crayon. As the black covering is scratched away, bright lines will appear almost like magic on the uniform blackness of the page. The lines are unpredictable in their colorfulness. All the randomness of the original coloring, beneath the equally random swoops of coin-scratch, result in wildly unusual shifts in shade and tone.

As an alternative to random squiggles and lines, you can, if you want, draw figures or houses or trees or flowers or whatever you like, with the edge of the coin. Either method will result in delightful, unpredictable color, and there is an endless fascination in drawing the coin along the grim flatness of the black page and watching a sparkling track of bright cheer dash along behind it.

There are only two problems with scratch drawings: finding enough black crayons (the black will used up long before anything else in the set) and finding enough fridge space to display the drawings. The shortage of black crayons may be second only to the shortage of black jelly beans as a major world problem!

Drip Painting

MATERIALS NEEDED: Large sheet of paper (18" × 24" is recommended), paint (mixed thinner than normal), paint brushes, several thicknesses of newspaper or anything else that will serve as a dropcloth

PLACE THE NEWSPAPER on the floor, which will be the kids' work surface, and place the paper on the newspaper. Have the kids stand over the paper.

Procedure: Dipping the paintbrushes into the runny, thin paint, let the color drip onto the paper and create patterns. That's all there is to it—the enjoyment of a different kind of art coupled with the pleasure of making a parent-sanctioned mess. You're not aiming to paint recognizable pictures—the results will definitely be abstract art!

Splatter Pictures

MATERIALS NEEDED: *Old toothbrush, old piece of window screen, paint (watercolors), thumbtacks, scissors, white cardboard, newspaper or anything else that will serve as a dropcloth*

SPREAD OUT NEWSPAPER not only thickly but widely—there's going to be a mess. You may even wish to see to it that the kids are wearing old clothes in case any paint gets on them, which is possible. You may need to lend a hand with this one.

Procedure: Cut any figure from a magazine or newspaper. Position it however you want on a piece of white cardboard, securing it with thumbtacks.

Hold the window screen about two inches above the cardboard. Dip the toothbrush into the paint and then rub it across the screen. The paint will spray through the openings in the screen onto the cardboard. You can do it all in one color or use several.

When the entire piece of cardboard has been sprayed, remove the thumbtacks and carefully remove the cut-out figure. The figure will have been silhouetted on the cardboard, with a splattered shading all around it.

Fingerprint Drawings

MATERIALS NEEDED: *Inkpad, paper, pencils or crayons or markers*

HERE'S ANOTHER PROJECT kids love as much because of the mess involved as because of the fun involved. It can produce some surprisingly interesting and creative results, but it will also be popular because it legitimizes their putting ink on their hands and then getting their fingerprints all over paper.

The least-messy approach to fingerprint art is to use a standard ink pad with washable ink. If pads of various colors are available at your local store, so much the better. As an alternative to the ink pad, if you want, it is possible to use a homemade ink pad, made from a paper towel folded several times over and soaked with tempera paint.

Your child may want to practice fingerprinting first, experimenting on a piece of scratch paper. S/he'll quickly learn that too much ink, or too much pressure, produces more of a mess than a pattern, blurring the whorls and loops and lines that make up a fingerprint. Once s/he gets the hang of it, don't be surprised if s/he gets sidetracked for a while, comparing fingerprints, seeing for himself/herself how no two are alike, and generally being amazed.

Once s/he's past the oh-wow stage, though, it's time to proceed to the real project at hand—if you'll pardon the pun. Now it's time to stop just having fun comparing fingerprints and generally making a mess, and to turn those fingerprints into art.

The most basic form of fingerprint drawing takes a single finger or thumb print and makes it the basis for some piece of drawn art. The oval shape of the ink smudge on the page offers some obvious suggestions: The print becomes a head or a face, the body of a cat or dog, the fuselage of an airplane—whatever suggests itself to your child.

Procedure: Working from the basic print, draw in details, or surround the print with representations of the world around the little print-person or print-dog or print-plane. Several fingerprints can be turned into a whole classroom full of heads. A five-finger set of prints can become a family. Prints can be combined to form the bases for elaborate pictures: three stacked vertically suggest a snowman; strung out horizontally, they become a dachshund, and so on. If different colors of ink are available, you can produce a tree trunk and branches in black or brown, then smudge green thumbprints above that to suggest clumps of leaves.

(Just don't let your child answer the phone or the doorbell till s/he's washed his or her hands!)

Foot Painting

MATERIALS NEEDED: *Newspapers, large sheets of white paper, buttermilk, tempera or fingerpaint*

SPREAD OUT THE newspaper over the floor for protection, and lay out the white paper on top of it. Pour ½ cup buttermilk onto the paper, and add ½ teaspoon tempera or fingerpaint. Now have your child sit on a chair at the edge of the paper. (His or her feet are going to get slippery; s/he's seated to avoid accidents.) Now, using feet and toes, s/he can paint the way s/he would do with fingerpaints, only using feet instead of hands. This is definitely a messy, fun project, and having a bucket of soapy water at hand, ready to wash the child's feet when s/he's done, is strongly recommended. It's also recommended that you make sure s/he doesn't have to go to the bathroom before starting, so s/he doesn't have to get up suddenly with blue and red feet, while painting!

Blow Paintings

MATERIALS NEEDED: *Tempera paint, paper (butcher paper is good), drinking straw*

THIS ART PROJECT will produce surprisingly attractive paintings of an abstract type. Tempera paint can be bought in powdered form, by the way, and mixed at home, which is cheaper than buying it already mixed. Art stores should have both kinds, and the premixed, at least, is available in many stationery stores.

Procedure: Put two or three small blobs of paint on the paper. Without touching the paint or the paper, blow through the straw, spreading the paint across the paper. Some control of the design's shape is possible, and some kids eventually become quite adept at manipulating the paint with their breathing.

The results are bright and cheerful and are a very nice alternative to coloring book pictures or pizza parlor placemats.

Paper Chains

MATERIALS NEEDED: *Magazines or construction paper, scissors, paste or glue or tape or stapler*

TO QUOTE A kindergarten teacher with forty years' experience behind her: "Kids *love* making chains!" Because the materials are so low-cost and the fun can keep the kids occupied for hours, parents love for kids to make chains, too.

Traditionally, chains have been made from construction paper, and of course they can be, but a couple of old magazines are really all that's necessary.

Procedure: Cut rectangular strips from magazine pages, producing roughly uniform pieces about an inch and a half wide and eight or nine inches long. Colored pictures—whether ads or whatever—are the best choice, but since making a chain is so much fun, most kids even enjoy making black-and-white chains.

Assembling the chains is easy: A strip of paper is curved into a circle, and a small dab of paste or glue holds the two overlapping ends together. (Joining the ends can also be accomplished with tape or staples, if the kids are old enough to use staples.) The second strip of paper is passed through the first link, then the ends are glued together to turn it into a circle. Then the next, and so on. (An industrious seven-year-old can easily create a chain fifteen or twenty feet long in no more time than it usually takes to mess up the living room or to open every jar in the spice rack.)

MOMMY, THERE'S NOTHING TO DO!

These chains can festoon your room, decorate the house for a birthday party, or even be worn around your neck as a necklace.

Yarn Play

MATERIALS NEEDED: *Pieces of yarn of any length, paper, glue, pencil or crayons*

A REMARKABLE ARRAY of creative and time-consuming activities can be found in a bag full of leftover pieces of yarn. In fact, if a parent is knitting a sweater, the child can spend the same time working with the same materials Mom (or Dad!) is.

Procedures for various projects:

- Draw a picture and then use yarn to turn it into a three-dimensional work of art. Frustration will be kept to a minimum if the drawing is done on a relatively large scale—14"x17" sheets are ideal. The people in the drawing can be fitted out with yarn hair, moustaches, and beards. Dogs can have yarn tails, yarn ears, yarn collars. Trees can bloom with puffy green branches or drooping willow leaves. Ground and grass are easily made with brown and green yarn, and snippets of yellow can be turned into lighted lamps or glowing fireflies. Yarn can make belts, hatbands, suspenders, and the trim on dresses. The possibilities are endless.
- In the reverse of the above activity, glue lengths of yarn to a page in no particular pattern, then turn

these random shapes and lines of yarn into pictures, using crayons or pencil to fill in the missing lines needed to form the pictures.

This variation requires that glue or paste be dispensed from a squeeze bottle with a fairly controllable dispensing tip. Draw a picture or pattern with the glue, making sure the line is thin, then lay the yarn along the line of glue. Be careful not to squeeze out too many lines of glue at a time, before placing the yarn down, to prevent the glue from drying before the yarn is laid down.

Many parents, as well as kids, will be surprised to discover what a number of hours of entertainment, quiet, and growing creativity are lurking in the bottom of the knitting basket.

Cardboard Jewelry

MATERIALS NEEDED: *Cardboard, scissors, paste, yarn, crayons or markers or paint. Optional: Glitter*

Procedure: Cut diamond shapes from pieces of cardboard. If you've got colored cardboard, great; if not, you can color plain gray cardboard with crayons or markers or paint. It's also possible to decorate the cardboard with glitter.

Now bend the diamond-shaped pieces in half over a piece of yarn that's the right length to make a kid-sized necklace or bracelet. After bending the pieces around the yarn, you'll be left with triangle shapes. Paste the pointed ends of the cardboard together, securing it on the yarn. You can use just one cardboard diamond or several or as many as will fit on the yarn, leaving room at the ends to tie them together around your wrist or neck.

Cork Necklaces

MATERIALS NEEDED: *Several corks, two brightly colored strings, large-eyed sewing needle*

SINCE A NEEDLE is used in this one, parental involvement is called for when younger kids try their hands at this.

Procedure: Thread one strand of brightly colored string through the needle, then pass the needle through the corks, spacing them as closely together or far apart as suits your sense of aesthetics. Now repeat the process using the other piece of string. Tie the ends of the strings together and you have a cork necklace.

Wildflower Necklace

MATERIALS NEEDED: *Wildflowers*

MAKING A WILDFLOWER necklace is not only fun but can improve a child's manual dexterity and give her or him experience in tying knots. The necklace won't last long, but the child will enjoy it while it does last.

Procedure: Pick a handful of wildflowers with long stems, then tie the bottom of one stem under the petals of another wildflower, and continue doing this till you have a completed circle of tied-together flowers of a size that will fit over your head in the style of a necklace.

Paper Beads

MATERIALS NEEDED: *Old magazines, scissors, glue, toothpicks or wooden matchsticks with the heads removed. For bracelets or necklaces: Dental floss, needle. For sewing onto doll clothes: Needle and thread. For pinning on: Safety pin*

Procedure: To make shiny and colorful beads, which can be strung, sewn, or pinned, cut long triangle shapes from colorful magazine pages. The proportion of the triangles should be like that of a pennant, and the length of the short end should be approximately equal to that of the toothpicks or matchsticks, whichever is being used. A dedicated bead-maker can consume a good hour just cutting the pieces from which this decorative paper jewelry will be made.

Place a toothpick or matchstick along the fat end of the pennant shape and roll the paper tightly around the stick. (Most children will soon develop skill at forming this bead shape remarkably quickly.)

When the entire triangle shape is rolled, place a small dab of glue over the pointed end, sealing and finishing the bead. When the stick is withdrawn, the bead is finished. Set it aside till you have rolled as many beads as you want.

These glisteningly colorful beads can be turned into necklaces or bracelets by threading a needle with dental floss, after which you can string them in whatever color sequence appeals to your sense of aesthetics. Or they can be pinned on clothes, hair ribbons, or tennis shoes with a safety pin, or sewn onto doll clothes.

Maybe you can't buy Manhattan for a pile of beads anymore, but kids can still have fun with them.

Macaroni Jewelry

MATERIALS NEEDED: Elbow macaroni, food coloring, string or dental floss

THIS IS ANOTHER activity in which parental help will almost surely be needed. For starters, you can avoid some mess and frustration with this craft if you'll prepare it for or with your child a day in advance. Dye a couple of handfuls of dry elbow macaroni with food color, producing as many colors as are available.

It's simple to achieve variations in the shades. Place a small number of uncolored elbows in a small container, such as the lid of a spice jar or vitamin bottle, and squeeze a few drops of undiluted food coloring onto the macaroni. Stir the elbows (a toothpick works fine for this), and you'll have vividly green or red or blue (or whatever) elbows.

Now carefully add enough warm water to fill the lid.

Swirl the lid to rinse off excess dye, then drain the colored water into a small bowl. The few elbows that were originally colored by the undiluted color will be much more vibrantly and strongly colored than the rest.

Next put a workable number of elbows into the bowl, add a few drops of coloring, then add warm water till the elbows are all covered. If the color has become too pale due to being too diluted, add a few more drops of the food coloring. Swish and swirl the bowl to make sure all the surfaces of the elbows have been dyed to some extent. Drain the water into another bowl, add more elbows, and restore the color with more drops of dye.

You'll probably find that you can create at least three distinct shades of each color—say, deep red, red, and pink—with the easily controlled technique of adding more dye or more water.

Here's why a day's advance work is a good idea: When you spread the macaroni out to dry (on something like waxed paper), you'll find that plenty of elbows that are dry to the touch still contain a drop or two of coloring inside them, drops that will make a distressing mess if your child begins her or his jewelry-making shortly after the dyeing procedure, before these last drops have had a chance to dry.

Now the project is ready for your child, though you may need to step in again later—we'll get to that in a minute.

Procedure: Separate the various colors of elbows; egg cartons are good for this, or just use bowls. String the brightly colored elbows on string or, even better, dental floss. Floss is strong and doesn't tend to fray as quickly as ordinary string.

Now here's where the child may need parental help again: Urging the string through the curved tube of the macaroni elbow can sometimes be frustrating. If so, the parent can help by lighting a candle, waiting a minute, then dipping the last inch or so of the string into the melted wax around the flame. This gives the string a sort of shoelace-end effect, which will make the stringing easier.

You can make long necklaces, short necklaces, bracelets, anklets, wall decorations, or Christmas tree ornaments. You can even make a brooch for Grandma by dyeing a two-inch length of paper drinking straw, stringing a loop of dyed elbows to match, and threading the string through the straw. The result is a colored horizontal bar (the straw) with a short loop of "gems" (the elbows). The whole thing can be pinned to a blouse without much trouble. It's fun to experiment with different patterns and color combinations. You'll find, too, that there can be as much variety achieved in varying the three different shades of one color as in mixing and matching totally different colors.

String Art Design Center

MATERIALS NEEDED: *One square of ¾"-thick plywood, measuring 18" × 18", small brads with round heads, hammer, one or two packages of stretchy fabric loops such as are used on children's weaving looms. (Don't substitute rubber bands; they can break and cause injury)*

THIS ACTIVITY WILL keep kids amused for hours, once you've prepared it. Do that by pounding the brads into the board so they're spaced one inch apart on the board and are all hammered in to the same depth. Now it's ready for your child.

Procedure: Stretch the fabric bands over the brads to create interesting designs, similar to string art. By varying the colors, you can form intricate abstract designs, or you can place the bands in such a way that they produce a "picture" of a house, a tree, a boat, or whatever.

The picture can be "erased" by removing and storing the loops till you want to "draw" on the string board again.

Mock Stained Glass Pictures

MATERIALS NEEDED: *Small piece of lightweight cardboard (such as the backing from a legal notepad), piece of aluminum foil a couple of inches larger than the cardboard, plastic wrap, cut slightly larger than the foil, tape, watercolor markers*

Procedure: Crumple the foil so it wrinkles, and use it to cover the cardboard. Tape it in place. Secure the plastic wrap to the table or desk top with tape. Outline the desired design with black marker, then fill it in with colored marker. When the picture is completed, lift up the wrap and tape it carefully over the foil.

Some designs seem especially suited to this activity—for example, colorful Christmas designs, bright spring flowers, and autumn cornucopias.

You can also use a variation on this method to produce small Christmas tree ornaments by cutting the cardboard to the desired shape, round or otherwise, and tracing around it on the plastic wrap before covering it with foil. With a large heavy needle, run a loop of thread through the top to form a hanger.

Collages

MATERIALS NEEDED: *Paper, paste or glue, cardboard or construction paper, varied items such as leaves, photographs, old greeting cards—use your imagination*

COLLAGES CAN BE as simple as autumn leaves or spring buds pasted on a sheet of construction paper or cardboard, or can be multimedia, involving natural items such as flowers, old photos (a great use for some of those shots that didn't quite come out right), and objects found around the house, such as extra buttons or empty spools of thread, or the "popcorn" that is used for cushioning packages in mailing, or uncooked macaroni.

For small children, the simplest of collages can be fashioned by having them paste or glue overlapping pieces of paper on construction paper, perhaps with a parent cutting the pieces of paper into interesting shapes for them. These can be intermixed with paste-on stars, for instance, or whatever is lying around that seems suitable.

Older kids can be more creative, exploring the house and the outdoor environment for suitable objects to paste on the collage, and using scissors to creatively cut interesting shapes out of wrapping paper saved off presents from Christmas or birthdays past, cut up parts of old photos, scraps of material or old clothes you were planning to consign to the dust rag pile, etc. Glitter can also be strategically added to the collage if desired.

Collages are a great way to constructively use old Christmas cards you might otherwise throw out, or birthday or other greeting cards. Collages made from this year's old Christmas cards, possibly intermixed with cut-up used Christmas gift wrap, can be used next year as Christmas decorations around the house.

Themed Collages

MATERIALS NEEDED: *Magazines and newspapers and any other media suitable for cutting up such as old greeting cards or photos that didn't come out quite right, scissors, paste or glue, construction paper or cardboard*

ANY COLLAGE CAN be fun to put together, but themed collages can be special and can also get your child thinking. The choice of theme can be your child's, or you can suggest one to get him/her started. Possible themes can be the seasons, animals, celebrations, or even emotions.

For a happy collage, for example, the child can choose pictures of happy people, or of things that make him/her feel happy. But don't just concentrate on happy thoughts. It's important for younger children to recognize the different emotions they feel, so sad and angry collages would be a good idea, too. Other possibilities exist such as excited or surprised as well as any other emotions your child is old enough to recognize, though it should be pointed out that happy will be the easiest emotion to find suitable pictures for, and the picture search will get progressively harder from there.

Younger kids may want to create alphabet collages,

with one sheet comprised of pictures of objects beginning with the letter *A*, another for *B*, and so forth, along with large-size examples of the letters themselves cut out from advertisements, article titles, or magazine covers. There is no limit to the topics a themed collage can cover—no limit, that is, except the child's imagination and the materials on hand.

Plaster Tile Carving

MATERIALS NEEDED: *Small cardboard box, petroleum jelly, plaster of Paris, knife or sharp carving instrument, pencil, clear acrylic finish*

THIS IS DEFINITELY a project for the older set, especially with the knife involved. It also needs to be prepared a day ahead.

Procedure:
First day: Coat the inside of the box with a thin layer of the petroleum jelly. Then prepare the plaster of Paris according to the instructions on the package and pour it into the box, letting it dry overnight.

Next day: Draw a design on the plaster lightly with a pencil. Then carve the design along the lines, with the knife or other carving tool, then paint it. When it's dry, spray it with a clear acrylic finish, and, when thoroughly dry, remove the finished tile from the box.

Stained Glass Windows

MATERIALS NEEDED: *One piece of onionskin typing paper, one piece of colored construction paper, colored markers, glue, scissors*

Procedure: Cut out various irregularly shaped pieces from the construction paper, not cutting all the way to the edge in any case. Carefully remove the pieces, without disturbing what remains of the paper. Now glue the typing paper to the back of the construction paper and, using different colors of markers, color in the shapes.

Hang it on a sunny window and let the light stream through.

Tissue Paper Flowers

MATERIALS NEEDED: *Four squares of same-size tissue paper, pipe cleaner*

Procedure: Place all four squares of paper together and fold them all like an accordion, with the folds close together. Taking the end of the pipe cleaner, wrap it around the middle of the folded papers. Now gently separate each sheet of tissue paper, starting from the top. (These will become the inside.) Do one side, then the other, adjusting as necessary to round the flower out.

Cloth Pictures

MATERIALS NEEDED: *Scraps of cloth, scissors, tagboard or old file folders, glue, pencils or crayons*

SMALLER CHILDREN WILL need help with the preliminaries, which involve cutting fabric scraps into various shapes. Depending on the fabric, even older children may need help with the cutting. The cutouts should include plenty of circles, triangles, rectangles, and squares, as well as a few odd shapes.

Show the child how the cloth can be laid out to make pictures: circles for heads, squares for bodies, triangles or trapezoids for dresses or skirts, squares for buildings, triangles for peaked roofs, long, thin, upright rectangles for tree trunks, and odd shapes for treetops. But of course the child doesn't have to limit himself or herself to just those possibilities. Encourage imaginativeness. (Ovals and rectangles make a great dachshund!)

Gluing the cloth to the tagboard is easy, unless you've cut out something nubby or texturey like tweed, and detail-minded kids may want to use pencil or crayons to fill in parts of the picture that haven't been taken care of by the fabric, though this isn't strictly necessary.

As a bonus, younger kids can use this activity as an exercise to help them distinguish among the basic shapes.

Seed Mosaics

MATERIALS NEEDED: *Assortment of seeds and similar items such as dry beans, probably including popcorn kernels, split peas, lentils, rice, brown rice, sunflower seeds, pumpkin seeds, and whatever else is around the house or available; also cardboard, glue, pencil, muffin tin or egg carton*

MOST PARENTS ARE surprised to discover how many elements of a seed mosaic are already lurking in their kitchen cupboards. While your child starts the project by drawing a picture on cardboard (landscapes are recommended here, rather than pictures of people), the parent prepares the next step by putting a spoonful of each kind of available seed or bean into the cups of a muffin tin or an egg carton.

Procedure: After finishing the drawing, decide what colors and textures to use for the various parts of the picture. Lentils make great ground or mountains, and peas will serve nicely for oceans, trees, and grass, to give you an idea. Now spread a small amount of glue over an area about the size of a half-dollar, and begin adding color and texture to the original art by placing seeds onto the glue. Continue till the entire picture has been completed, with beans and seeds and such as the medium depicting the scenery.

It might be useful to keep a damp washcloth nearby

to wash off any glue that might get on your fingers during the placing of the seeds.

It's possible to frame and hang seed paintings, which make great gifts for Grandma and Grandpa.

Pussywillow Art

MATERIALS NEEDED: *Pussywillows, paper, glue, pencils or crayons. Optional: Jellybeans, cotton*

OF COURSE PUSSYWILLOWS are fun to touch and hold and stroke, enjoying the catlike furriness, but they have a place in crafts projects, too.

Procedure: A small dab of glue will hold a pussywillow onto a piece of paper. The classic project is to draw a picture of a cat, using the pussywillow as the cat's body, filling in the rest of the picture with pencil, crayons, or for that matter any other medium. The cat might be sitting on a fence, with the fence drawn in under the oval pussywillow, and the hanging-down tail drawn, too. The head and ears can be drawn as well, or if you have smaller pussywillow buds, they can be used for the head and ears.

For a larger drawing, paste any number of pussywillows densely together to form the body of a larger cat.

But the pussywillow doesn't have to represent a cat's body; it can also be a rabbit, a beard on a comical face, or a mythical creature the rest of whose body is drawn from your imagination. Two pussywillows can be slippers on a person's feet. In forming the body of a larger animal, you can use black jellybeans for the eyes, and if the animal is a rabbit, a puff of cotton can be pasted on for the tail.

The fun part is that, no matter how well the picture comes out, you're bound to have a good time just handling the pussywillows!

Mosaics

MATERIALS NEEDED: *Construction paper (as many colors as possible), scissors, paper or cardboard or tagboard, pencil, glue, egg carton*

MOSAICS ALMOST ALWAYS turn out very well, which makes the project that much more enjoyable for the kids. If the child is too young to cut out the shapes, a little parental help is in order.

Procedure: The first step is to cut colored construction paper into *small* pieces, mostly squares, rectangles, and triangles. The egg carton is for storing the cut-out pieces, keeping the triangles together, the squares together, etc.

The mosaic can be put together freehand, or a drawing can be made with pencil first, with the pieces laid down according to the pattern or drawing you've created. You can work on plain typing paper, or black or white construction paper, but the most durable is heavy tagboard or light- to medium-weight cardboard.

If you've drawn a picture in pencil, fill in the outlines now with the little pieces of paper, patchworking them in till the drawing is completely filled in. Spread glue over a small area at a time, to prevent it from drying in some areas before you get to them and for minimization of mess. You can decide what shapes and what colors to use in which parts of the drawing. (Two kids working on the same drawn outline will come up with totally different mosaics if left to their own choices of color and shape.)

Mosaics can be hung, framed and hung, or used to replace pictures under glass on serving trays.

Soap Sculpture

MATERIALS NEEDED: *Bar of soap, paring or pocket knife*

BECAUSE THIS PROJECT involves carving with a knife, we are of course talking about older kids here. The kids must be mature enough and skilled enough to control a knife safely and to do detailed work carefully. Soap carving is very satisfying once you get the hang of it.

The large-size bar of Ivory is recommended for the soap: It's firm enough to carve without being too hard, it doesn't crumble, and the white color suggests marble.

For the thrifty or ecologically minded parent, it's possible to rescue the shavings when the child is done, mash those shavings together, and use them for the purpose the soap bar was originally intended.

When the carving is finished, shallow grooves can be cut across the bottom of the sculpture, then the sculpture can be fitted over a pair of Popsicle sticks. Now the soap statue can stand up and be put on display.

Vase

MATERIALS NEEDED: *Small wide-mouthed jar, white glue, various colors of yarn, small paintbrush*

Procedure: Starting at the bottom of the outside of the jar, paint an approximately one-inch-high strip of white glue all around the jar. Now slowly wrap the yarn around the jar, keeping the rows tight to each other so you can't see the glue or the jar between strands of yarn. When that first inch of glue is almost covered, apply another inch of glue. (It's better not to cover the entire glued area before applying more glue, because otherwise it's too easy to smear the fresh glue on the yarn.) When the next inch of glue has been applied, more yarn goes on. As you apply the yarn to the jar, press down on the yarn to make sure it's firmly anchored in the glue. Continue working in one-inch sections till the whole outside of the jar is covered, changing colors as often as suits your sense of aesthetics.

After the glue has dried, the yarn should be painted with a mixture of half white glue and half water to give the vase a shiny finish, and then it should be left to dry overnight.

Tissue Paper Sun Catchers

MATERIALS NEEDED: *String, white glue, tissue paper of various colors, scissors, water, pencils*

YOU'LL PROBABLY WANT to work on this one with your kids, at least the younger ones, and maybe even the older ones till they get the hang of it.

Procedure: In a bowl, mix the glue with a little bit of water to thin it slightly. Cut the string into workable lengths of about two feet and place it in the bowl, making sure it's thoroughly covered by the glue solution. Lightly draw a design on the tissue paper with the pencil. The best designs for this are simple ones such as butterflies, hearts, circles, or stars.

Now remove the string from the glue solution and squeeze the excess moisture from it by running it between two fingers. Carefully place the string along the pencil lines on the tissue paper, pressing it down as you go to be sure it adheres properly. Place a second sheet of tissue paper on top of the string and press down.

After it's dry, carefully trim the two sheets of paper around the design with a scissors. The string will remain stiff and keep the shape of the design.

Now it can be hung in the window to catch the sun in the color of the tissue paper.

Yarn-Ball Holder

MATERIALS NEEDED: *Oatmeal box, paper, glue, paints or markers or crayons*

THE EXTRA PLEASURE in this project is that not only is it fun to work on, but the end result is a useful object, not just an attractive one.

Procedure: Decorate the outside of an oatmeal box by covering it with paper you've painted or drawn on. Brown paper (such as from a grocery bag), several glued- or taped-together pieces of typing paper, or a large sheet of construction paper can be used to cover the box. It's easier to do the drawing, coloring, or painting on the paper before it's attached to the box, so the paper should be measured and cut to size, or small sheets glued or taped together, if need be, then laid down on a table to be drawn or painted on.

Cut a hole an inch in diameter into the center of the lid of the oatmeal box. The ball of yarn stays in the box, the end drawn through the lid, and now the ball of yarn won't scramble all over the floor while Grandma is knitting. What a great birthday present for any knitter (or crocheter) in the family!

Decorative Container

MATERIALS NEEDED: *Empty coffee can, glue, scissors, colored felt, magazines. Optional: Glitter*

RELATED IN CONCEPT to the above project is the decorative container, usable as a pencil holder, marbles or jacks holder, or as a container for any other odds 'n' ends.

Procedure: Cut one large strip of felt of a size to cover the entire coffee can, then cut out shapes from the remaining felt (preferably of a different color), along with magazine pictures, and glue the felt cutouts and magazine pictures to the big piece of felt on the can. If desired, you can then add strategically placed glitter. Give the glue holding the cutouts to the felt a few minutes to dry. Then glue the large piece of felt and place it on the coffee can. When dry, it's ready to be used or given as a gift.

Pomander Balls

MATERIALS NEEDED: *Apple, whole cloves, netting, yarn*

THIS ONE'S EASY, and the scent it'll give off makes it a pleasure to work on.

Procedure: Stick the cloves into the apple about a quarter inch apart; then wrap the apple in the netting. Gather the netting and tie it at the top with the yarn, leaving a loop in the yarn for hanging.

Hung in an open area of the room, the pomander ball will give off a fresh, sweet/sharp scent.

Mobiles

MATERIALS NEEDED: *Nylon thread, supports such as dowel rods and/or hangers, scissors, glue or paste, material for making suspended objects (cardboard, straws, paper, heavy material, wire)*

Procedure: Find or make objects to hang from the mobile. These can be cut-out pictures pasted to cardboard, which is then cut around the picture, or cardboard or even heavy material that has been drawn on by the child. In fact, the only limitation on what can be hung is that it be strong enough to support something else possibly hanging from it, and lightweight enough that it doesn't cause the mobile to fall.

A really simple mobile might consist merely of a hanger with nylon thread suspended from each end and something hanging from each piece of nylon thread. Multilevel mobiles are trickier but more fun. For instance, hang a dowel from each end of a hanger or larger dowel, with an object hanging from each end of each dowel. How many tiers are constructed will depend on your patience and your skill in balancing objects to keep the mobile from tipping.

Rock Paperweights

MATERIALS NEEDED: *Smooth rocks, paints or markers*

SMOOTH, ROUNDED ROCKS on the medium-to-large side can be decorated by children of any age and presented to relatives and friends for use as decorative paperweights. Collecting appropriate pretty rocks can be an ongoing project or the specific purpose of an afternoon's expedition.

Procedure: Rinse off the rocks and dry them; dust or dirt will interfere with the paint or marker.

If the rock isn't a particularly pretty color, you may want to paint the entire rock white first, but this isn't mandatory. You can decorate it by painting a design, a miniature landscape (on a fairly large rock), a face, swirls, or the initials of the intended recipient. Painting can be done with watercolors, acrylics, or markers.

Pieces of Rainbows

MATERIALS NEEDED: *Five-inch embroidery hoop, fabric, embroidery needle, assorted colors of thread, sixteen-inch piece of lace or eyelet edging, glue*

EVEN A CHILD who does not yet have the fine motor skills necessary to do ordinary cross-stitching can produce a special gift for a parent or grandparent, as long as the child is old enough to use a needle responsibly. (Parental help in threading the needle may be called for.)

The fabric should be stretched tightly in a five-inch embroidery hoop, as if for cross-stitching. The best color choices for the cloth are unobtrusive ones such as pale blue, light pink, pale yellow, light beige, or white; you and your child might want to select the fabric on the basis of the decor of the intended recipient.

Procedure: Sew single stitches, long or short, in whatever patterns appeal to you, selecting the colors, and deciding where to place the stitches. The different-colored stitches are the pieces of rainbows.

When you are satisfied that there are enough pieces of rainbows on the cloth, glue the strip of edging around the back of the rim of the embroidery hoop. You now have a stretched, framed-in-lace, colorful little bit of personalized stitchery, suitable for hanging on Grandma's (or your own) wall.

Walnut Mice

MATERIALS NEEDED: *Walnut shells, felt scraps (black, brown, or gray), glue, scissors, yarn (black, brown, or gray), black marker, bristles from an old brush or broom*

Procedure: Glue a four inch piece of yarn to one end of half a walnut shell; this is the mouse's tail. Cut ears and a nose from the felt and glue these to the other end. Use the marker to make two eyes. The bristles of an old brush or broom provide the whiskers; two should be glued to each side of the nose. You now have a walnut mouse.

Sand Paper Art

MATERIALS NEEDED: *Colored construction paper, white glue, colored sand, spoon*

Procedure: With the glue, draw a picture or design on the construction paper. Possibilities include abstract designs, initials or full names, simple pictures such as a face or the outline of an animal, or landscapes or even more complex pictures.

Using the spoon, sprinkle the sand over the glue till

the glue is well covered. After shaking off the excess sand, let the glue dry. The project is completed.

As a variation, you can use more than one color of sand. Let the glue dry after using one color before putting down the glue for the next color.

Potpourri Sachet

MATERIALS NEEDED: *Dried flowers, potpourri oil, thin cotton fabric (preferably printed rather than solid), ribbon*

Procedure: Pull the petals off the flowers. (If they do not come off easily, they need more time to dry.) The petals should then be sprinkled with a liberal amount of the oil. Now cut the fabric into a circle approximately six inches in diameter and place a small handful of the petals in the center of the fabric, pulling the cloth together and tying it with the ribbon, finally tying a decorative bow in the ribbon.

Creative Clothes

MATERIALS NEEDED: *Waterproof marker, T-shirt or sweatshirt, pencil, paper, pins*

Procedure: With pencil and paper, draw the design you want on the shirt, erasing and redrawing till you have it just the way you want. Then cut it out of the paper, creating a stencil. Pin the homemade stencil to the shirt and color the design onto the garment.

Iron-On Transfers

MATERIALS NEEDED: *One sheet of medium- or coarse-grain sandpaper, crayons (broken pieces work fine here), piece of fabric, piece of scrap cloth, iron*

KIDS LOVE CREATING their own holiday banners, clubhouse flags, and similar decorations with this fun technique.

Procedure: While the iron is preheating at the hottest setting, use the crayons to draw your design on the rough side of the sandpaper. It's recommended that beginners draw something simple like a flower or geometric pattern, only attempting more complicated images when they're more proficient. It's important to remember that letters or numerals need to be written backward in order for them to come out right-way-round on the finished product. It's also necessary to press hard when coloring the sandpaper so plenty of color sticks to the grain.

After the design is complete, place the decorated sandpaper facedown on the surface to which you want to transfer the design. The scrap cloth goes on top of the sandpaper to protect the iron. Now iron the scrap cloth for about thirty seconds, peel the sandpaper off the material on the bottom, and voila! Your creation is complete.

Tie Dyeing

MATERIALS NEEDED: *Fabric dye, clothes, rubber bands, newspaper, containers for dye*

Procedure: Mix the dye as directed, adding a pinch of salt if it's not already in the packaged dye. Cover the work surface and floor with newspaper for protection. Now gather the material of the clothing into bunches, held tightly with rubber bands. Dip the clothing into the dye. Let the clothing dry completely on the newspaper before removing the rubber bands, but wash the containers out immediately.

Loving Hands Sweatshirt

MATERIALS NEEDED: *One sweatshirt, fabric paint, disposable pie tins*

WHAT GRANDMOTHER WOULDN'T be proud to wear a sweatshirt that reminds her of the grandchild(ren) she loves? In a large family, this easy activity can involve all the grandchildren from all sides of the family; and even if the cousins can't get together at the same time to work on the shirt, the shirt can be mailed from family to family until each child has had a chance to add his or her own special touch. One Washington state grandmother recently received for Christmas a pale pink sweatshirt displaying the handprints of all five of her grandchildren, who live in three different states.

Begin by buying a sweatshirt in the appropriate size and favorite color of the grandma or other intended recipient. Then buy several bottles of washable fabric paint in coordinating shades. If several children are involved, a different color for each child is suggested. If Grandma only has one grandchild, two different colors are a good idea.

Squeeze the paint into the pie tins, and have the children put their hands into the paint and then, after letting excess paint drip back into the tin (don't let them shake their hands and "redecorate" the kitchen), onto the shirt.

If there's more than one child involved, each may want to sign his or her name below his or her handprint.

Silhouette Portraits

MATERIALS NEEDED: *Chair, bright light, sheet of white paper, thumbtacks, pencil, sheet of black paper, paste, sheet of white construction paper, scissors*

THIS ONE'S NOT for really little kids, as it involves a certain degree of manual dexterity.

Procedure: Thumbtack a sheet of white paper to a

wall, and seat your model near the paper on the wall, placing a bright light (preferably from a bare bulb) on the opposite side of the model. If there isn't a clear shadow of the model cast on the sheet of paper mounted on the wall, adjust the light or the model's position.

Now outline the shadow cast on the paper, using a pencil. Then cut out that outline and place it on a sheet of black paper. Trace around that and cut it out, then mount the black silhouette on a sheet of white construction paper, and you have a silhouette portrait.

Hanger Faces

MATERIALS NEEDED: *Wire coat hanger, stocking or panty hose, construction paper or typing paper, scissors, crayons, paste, pin or string. Optional: Cotton, pipe cleaners, buttons, etc.*

Procedure: Bend a coat hanger into a circle, then carefully stretch the leg of an old stocking over the wire. When the fabric of the stocking is pulled tightly along the rim of the circle, gather the loose material and fasten it with a pin or string around the neck of the hanger hook.

You now have a tightly stretched circle of nylon fabric, ready to turn into a comical face. Eyes, a nose, and a mouth can be drawn on, or cut out from magazine pictures and pasted on, or drawn on a separate sheet of construction paper and pasted on. Or they can be created out of scraps of material or other items found around the house. Example: A chestnut can be a goofy nose; yarn can make a mouth.

The hanger faces can get as elaborate as you want: cotton or yarn or loose hair from a toothbrush for hair or a beard, pipe cleaners bent into eyeglasses, and so forth. Ready-made googly eyes are available at many crafts stores, if desired.

With cotton and red construction paper or crepe paper, you can fashion Santa and Mrs. Claus. And of course, these hanger faces are easy to hang and display, since the hanging hooks are built right in!

Jeweled Egg Ornaments

MATERIALS NEEDED: *Eggs, heavy darning needle, sequins, egg hangers or stands (available at craft shops), disinfectant, water, Elmer's Glue. Optional: Manicure scissors, small figurines, narrow lace trim*

THESE ORNAMENTS LOOK rich enough to rival the real thing, but are actually covered with inexpensive sequins. They take some time to create, so they are not for children with minimal patience, but they're worth the effort.

Procedure: Shake the eggs carefully but vigorously. With the darning needle, poke a small hole in each end of each egg. Hold the egg over the sink or a bowl, cover one end of the egg with your mouth, and blow hard to force out the yolk and white. It'll take a minute to get the hang of it, but before long the eggs will be empty.

Next submerge the shells in a solution of disinfectant and water, and swish them around to make sure the water gets inside. After rinsing them under running water, set them aside to dry.

When they're fully dry, strengthen them by coating them with three coats of Elmer's Glue. Then glue on sequins and glitter. Finally, add the hanger, and you've created a beautiful keepsake ornament.

For an even more unusual effect, you can cut an opening in the front of the egg before it's glued. Then glue narrow lace or tiny beads around the opening and put small figurines inside. For example, you can create a Nativity scene. Or you can cut the egg in half with a small saw such as a Dremel tool and attach small hinges to make a ring box.

It is also possible to prime the eggs with a clear base coat, rather than using glue, and then paint them with acrylic paints.

Basket of Flowers

MATERIALS NEEDED: *Milkweed that's gone to seed, long-stemmed grasses or wild oats, spray paint, scissors, aerosol hair spray or clear shellac, wicker basket, ribbon*

THIS IS A project with which you'll need to lend a hand.

Since it's possible to turn trash into artwork, why not weeds? Choose earthy fall colors to create the perfect centerpiece for holiday table settings, or a basket in different shades of blue to set off a bathroom or bedroom. Wherever you put the finished product, your child will be proud to say, "I made it myself." You'll also be happy to know that it will last almost forever.

Procedure: Bring the spray paint and hair spray or shellac with you when you go out hunting for the milkweed and grasses. Start by finding a field full of milkweed that's gone to seed. Milkweed may be called by other names in different parts of the country, but you'll recognize it by its big, fluffy white seed heads, which resemble a dandelion after it's turned white. While you're out there, look for some long-stemmed grasses or wild oats, as well. There's a good chance they'll be growing in the same field as the milkweed.

Carefully spray the seed heads with paint, keeping the nozzle several inches from the plant so the force of the spray won't blow the seed head away. While the milkweed is drying, spray the grasses or wild oats with two or three light coats of hair spray.

When everything is dry, cut the painted milkweed and grasses with the long stems. Transport them home carefully, and when you get there, arrange them in baskets, tying them with a ribbon in a complementary color. If desired, you can also buy dried baby's breath from a florist or crafts shop to add variety to your arrangement.

Some tried-and-true color combinations to keep in mind are brown-yellow-orange in a dark basket for fall arrangements, different shades of blue in a light cream-colored basket, or lighter shades of pink with wine or burgundy and touches of pale blue.

Miscellaneous Activities

Secret Codes and Ciphers

MATERIALS NEEDED: *Pencil and paper*

ONE OF THE most satisfying skills a child can acquire is the ability to communicate secretly, whether it is for the purpose of sending a message to a friend or for keeping a diary for her or his own self. Either way, s/he knows no moms or little brothers or sisters can intercept these top-secret communications.

Ciphers and codes are very flexible, the simplest readily available to children almost as soon as they can read, the more complex baffling even to adults. Here are some ciphers and codes that kids will enjoy working with.

In the simplest number-for-letter substitution codes, *1* represents *A*, *2* represents *B*, and so forth. The child and his/her friend know what the code is, and can easily translate the letters of words into numbers and back again to decode the coded message and encode replies or new messages. A slightly more complicated code starts *1* somewhere other than *A:* If *C = 1,* then *D = 2,* and *E = 3,* and so forth. Or if *L = 1,* then *M = 2* and *N = 3.* This is a little harder for an intercepting child (or parent) to decode.

Carrying the complication one step further, the numbers don't have to follow in sequence at all, but can be assigned to letters in random order. Arbitrarily, *A* could be *5, B* could be *23, C* could be *16,* and so forth. The child prints the alphabet on two pieces of paper, being sure to leave space immediately beneath each letter on both sheets of paper. The child then assigns a number to each letter, writing the same numbers under the letters on both sheets of paper. One copy of the code is for himself/ herself; the other is for the friend with whom s/he will be communicating.

It is not even necessary to restrain the code to the first twenty-six numbers. *A* could be *31* if the child wanted. Such a code is much harder to break, as the numbers do not follow in any logical order.

If the child can remember the sentence "J. Q. SCHWARTZ FLUNG D. V. PIKE MY BOX," then s/he has the key to a great substitution code. There are exactly twenty-six letters in that sentence, and if you number them in order, *J = 1, Q = 2, S = 3,* and so forth, you have a rememberable key to the code, even if you lose the piece of paper it's written on.

It's also possible to substitute one letter for another, rather than using numbers. In the simplest code, one letter is substituted for the next one down the line, so that *A = B, B = C, C = D,* and so forth. Another easy system is to write the alphabet forward, then write it again backward underneath that, so that *A = Z, B = Y, C = X,* and so on. But, as with the number substitutions, it is not necessary to go in order. Random assignments of letters (*A = M, B = F, C = U,* for instance) provide a harder code to crack.

Face Painting

MATERIALS NEEDED: *Muffin tin, and, for each color of paint: 1 teaspoon cornstarch, ½ teaspoon water, ½ teaspoon cold cream, a few drops of food coloring*

IT'S EASY FOR kids to put on a happy face with this easy-to-make, easy-to-use, easy-to-remove face paint. Your child can wear it to fairs and carnivals, as a fun way of celebrating holidays, and when staging plays for friends and family. It comes off easily with cold cream and tissues.

Mix the ingredients shown above, using the various cups of the muffin tin for the various colors. A small paintbrush works well for applying the paint. Possibilities for patterns are a clown face, a rainbow on each cheek and/or the forehead, a circle of hearts for Saint Valentine's Day, tiny shamrocks on each cheek for Saint Patrick's Day, or stars and stripes for the Fourth of July.

If the kids want to play zoo, they can turn themselves into zebras, leopards, or tigers with striped or spotted makeup.

Alphabetizing Books

MATERIALS NEEDED: *Books*

THIS ACTIVITY WILL not only keep your child busy for a while, but it will also give him or her a feeling of responsibility for his/her books, instill a feeling for organization, and give him or her some excellent practice in the skills of alphabetizing.

Nothing could be more basic: The child arranges the books on his/her bookshelf alphabetically. You may need to explain that, traditionally, the word *The* as the first word of a title is ignored for the purposes of alphabetizing. You may also need to help, especially with a younger child, prompting, "Which comes first, *L* or *I?* Say your alphabet."

For a younger child, it may be enough just to put the *A*'s together, the *B*'s together, and so forth, but most young children don't have that many books, and full alphabetizing of his or her collection should be possible even for some younger kids and certainly for all older ones. If kids want to alphabetize by author instead, by all means let them. There's no reason to insist on one system over the other.

Older kids who are great book lovers and have more extensive libraries may even want to divide their books by category, putting dinosaur books together, rock collecting books together, and so forth, or merely separating fiction from nonfiction. (If your child isn't familiar with those two terms, now's a great time to explain them.) Real book lovers may even want to make themselves a card catalog of sorts! A recipe box is perfect for this purpose.

Drawing a Family Tree

MATERIALS NEEDED: *Paper and pen or pencil*

DRAW A FAMILY tree. How complicated you make it, and how many generations back you want to go will depend on how knowledgeable you are about your family history and how much time you want to put into this project. But at very least go back to the kids' grandparents.

For younger kids from a large family with lots of aunts, uncles, and cousins, it can sometimes be confusing to get it straight: Who's related how? Having it on paper will make it easier to understand, because it's visible in the form of a drawing.

A good place to keep the family tree is in the family photo album, where you can show the kids pictures of many (if not all) of the people on the tree. As well as drawing the tree, it's nice if you can write a family history to keep with the tree, telling about when ancestors may have come from another country, what grandparents did for a living, and as much other interesting information as you can gather together. Not only will this be interesting to the kids now, it will be particularly meaningful to them twenty-five years from now when they're grown up and have kids of their own, and some of the people on the family tree are no longer around to provide answers to questions like, "What was Grandma's Grandma's name?" or "Where did Great-Grandpa go to school?"

Family Time Line

MATERIALS NEEDED: *Strip of paper 12 inches wide by several feet long, markers*

TAPE THE TIME line along one wall of the child's bedroom or in a hallway. Begin the time line as far back in time as your memory or other available data will allow. For instance, you can start with the year your grandmother was born. After the beginning date, divide the time line into set increments, perhaps ten years. As you get nearer to the present time, you may wish to use increments of one year. Mark each increment with the appropriate date, then begin to add significant data about each family member, such as birthdates, marriages, graduations, etc.

Place each child's name and birthdate on the time line, then show them the time span between their birthday and, say, yours or your grandparents', or their siblings'. To help your child begin to understand the passage of time and develop a perspective about history, you might also record other significant events that have occurred during his/her lifetime, especially ones s/he'll remember: A favorite vacation, the year s/he got his/her bike, the year s/he began school. All these events will help put terms like "one year ago" into a comprehensible perspective.

You can add new sections to the time line as the

years pass. Be sure to save the old sections, too, though; they'll provide precious family history for your grandchildren some day.

Literal Family Tree or Theme Tree

MATERIALS NEEDED: *Three- to four-foot branch approximately one inch in diameter that has many forks and twigs projecting from it, small bucket or wastebasket filled with dirt, yarn, family pictures, hole punch or pencil or scissors for punching holes*

PLACE THE BRANCH in the dirt-filled container, making sure it's secure.

For a family tree, cut the pictures into circles and punch a hole in the top of each picture, then string a piece of nylon through each hole and tie each picture to a different fork or twig. For a more artistic appearance, vary the colors of yarn used. For simplicity and uniformity, use all the same color.

For a theme tree, substitute theme pictures for family pictures. Possible themes include favorite sports, sports heroes, holidays, animals, summer vacation pictures, friends, cars, dinosaurs, or any other topic of interest to your child or children. The pictures can be photos, pictures cut from magazines, or ones drawn by the kids themselves.

Flags

MATERIALS NEEDED: *Paper, crayons or markers*

IF POSSIBLE, IT'S nice for this activity to follow a look through the "Flags" entry in the encyclopedia. Even if you don't have an encyclopedia at home and don't feel like taking a trip to the library, you and your kids can discuss how the colors and designs on flags often are symbolic of some special quality or characteristic. (Examples: The Southern Cross on Australia's flag signifies its location in the southern hemisphere; Canada's maple leaf is its national symbol; the Star of David on Israel's flag represents the country's identity as the Jewish homeland; the diagonal red bars on Florida's flag are a reminder of the state's participation in the Confederacy.)

Now have your child design his or her own personal flag, choosing whatever colors, patterns, symbols, or designs seem appropriate. S/he'll enjoy explaining the details of the flag to you, and having the flag decorating his or her room.

Leaf Collection

MATERIALS NEEDED: *Large bag, leaves (to be gathered)*

GATHERING LEAVES IS not exclusively an autumnal activity—and if that statement surprises you, you can learn just as much from this little trip as your child can.

Although older kids might set off around the neighborhood on their own, this is an activity that's especially rewarding as a time for parent and child to be together. The aim of the journey around the yard, the neighborhood, or the park is to gather a sample of every different kind of leaf.

Regardless of the child's age, there will be something to learn appropriate to that age. Very small kids can use this opportunity to notice for the first time the structure of leaves, including the stem or spine (the petiole), the blades (what we think of when we think of *leaf*), and the vein patterns. Older kids can begin to understand the concept of circulation of water and nutrients through the plant, or of photosynthesis and transpiration.

Other types of thinking and comprehension can be encouraged during leaf collection walks. Smaller kids can use the discussion to distinguish between plant and animal forms of life, and to describe features that are common to both plants and animals (they both can die, they both need some kind of food and drink), as against those peculiar to plants only or animals only (most animals can move from one spot or another, while plants are rooted in one place).

Older kids can recognize that some leaves are simple while others are compound, and that some have smooth edges while others are rough-edged or lobed.

On your return home, the leaf collection can be spread out on a table and organized however the child likes. If you know the names of all the varieties s/he's collected, s/he can glue or tape each leaf to a sheet of paper and label it with its name. Or the leaves can simply be arranged decoratively in a basket for pure pleasure.

Pressed Flowers

MATERIALS NEEDED: *Assorted fresh flowers and grasses, waxed paper, paper towels, heavy books*

THIS ACTIVITY IS a delightful way to preserve some of the beauty of summer, and is another activity you and your child can enjoy together. Pick an assortment of flowers and long-stemmed grasses, and spread them in a single layer between two sheets of paper towel. Wrap the towel with wax paper, then carefully slip the entire sheet between the pages of a heavy book. Set the book aside for about a month, and when you open it, you'll discover that the flowers are pressed and dried, beautifully preserved for future enjoyment.

Pressed Flowers in a Frame

MATERIALS NEEDED: *Pressed flowers and grasses, 3" × 5" canvas panel (available at arts and crafts stores), oval mat with 3" × 5" opening, 5" × 7" picture frame with glass, small piece of ribbon or yarn. Optional: Acrylic paints*

ONE WAY TO use pressed flowers is to turn them into a charming framed wall hanging that's the perfect addition to any room.

Procedure: Begin by laying the canvas on a table or other work surface. If desired, you can sponge on blue and white acrylic paint to form a "cloudy sky" background, but it's not essential to do so, as the unpainted canvas will also be very attractive.

Now arrange the flowers and grasses into a nice bouquet. Tie the stems together at the base with the ribbon or yarn, and glue the bouquet in place on the canvas in a few spots.

Since artists always sign their work, put your name or initials in one of the bottom corners.

Now carefully put the canvas inside the oval mat, and then into the frame. Presto! You've created the perfect gift—if you can bear to give it away.

Treasure in the Dust

MATERIALS NEEDED: *Coins, a dust cloth. Optional: Dusting spray or wax*

LET'S FACE IT—no matter what your age, it's hard to get excited about dusting the furniture. But a handful of change, even pennies, coupled with some ingenuity on the part of you, the parent, can provide plenty of incentive for kids who need to "clean up their act."

All you have to do is hide coins in various spots around the room—in the corners of shelves, under bric-a-brac and books, under lamps, and in any other hard-to-spot place. Make a few easy to find, but really hide the rest so your child will pick up objects to dust and not just go around them. After you've finished burying all the treasure, tell your child that any money s/he finds while dusting is his or hers to keep. Now turn the child loose with a soft cloth—and dusting spray or wax if you want him or her to use it—and you'll be surprised at how thoroughly s/he cleans as s/he searches for hidden treasure.

Thumbelina

MATERIALS NEEDED: *Ballpoint pen or fine-point washable marker, hankie or tissue or piece of cloth*

THIS AMUSES THE heck out of a three-year-old, according to one mom of seven kids, all of whom were three at one point or another. Draw a simple face, eyes, nose, and mouth, on your thumb (on both thumbs if you're ambidextrous). Wrap a hankie, tissue, or piece of cloth below the face. It will serve as a dress.

Mom's (or Dad's) thumb can talk to the child, probably in a charming or comical voice. If both thumbs have been drawn on, they can talk to each other. Thumbelina can have a funny conversation with the child just for amusement, of course; but she can also allay the child's fears if s/he is suddenly unwilling to submerge his/her face in the bath, talk to people, take a first trip to the dentist, or whatever. A good calming talk from Thumbelina can solve the problem.

Make a Recipe Box

MATERIALS NEEDED: *Shoebox, scissors, old newspapers and/or magazines, tape or paste, index cards*

AS SOON AS a child is old enough to cook simple foods, s/he can make his or her own recipe box, decorating an old shoe box with pictures of foods cut from old newspapers and magazines. Most major urban daily papers have a food section once a week, and virtually all publications have grocery ads or ads from major food companies, with illustrations of various foods.

The child can now write recipes on index cards, to be put in the shoe box. If s/he already has favorites s/he cooks, s/he can write them down on the index cards, copying from her cookbook or getting the instructions verbally from you. If you know any other simple-to-cook foods, now's a good time to give those recipes to your child for inclusion in the box—and for cooking at the next available opportunity, another activity to pass the time when your child says, "Mommy, there's nothing to do!"

Fruit Shakes

MATERIALS NEEDED: *Two cups cold juice, ½ cup powdered milk, ¼ teaspoon vanilla, a few ice cubes, measuring cups, measuring spoon, plastic shaker*

ONE RECIPE THAT can easily go into the recipe box (see page 147) is this one. Minimal adult supervision is needed, and the end result is a healthful treat.

Recipe: Pour two cups of chilled juice into a shaker. Any kind of fruit juice (not vegetable juice) will work fine. Add ½ cup powdered milk, ¼ teaspoon vanilla, and a few ice cubes.

Put the top *securely* on the shaker. Then shake like crazy till the mixture is smooth, pour into a tall glass, and enjoy.

This recipe can also be prepared in a blender.

Peanut Butter Candy

MATERIALS NEEDED: *One cup peanut butter, one cup corn syrup, 1¼ cups powdered milk, 1¼ cups powdered sugar, mixing bowl, wax paper, fork*

HERE'S ANOTHER RECIPE your child can make by himself/herself, for inclusion in that recipe box:

Combine all the ingredients in the mixing bowl, mix together, and roll into balls on the wax paper. The candy can be chilled or eaten at room temperature.

BOOKS FOR FAMILY LIFE

__STEPMOTHERING: ANOTHER KIND OF LOVE
Pearl Ketover Prilik 0-425-12050-3/$4.50
Stepfamily relationships are growing more common—yet the experience can still be a difficult one. This personal, positive approach offers intelligent and sensitive answers to a stepmother's everyday problems.

__GROWING UP HAPPY by Bob Keeshan
0-425-12315-4/$4.95
He brightened the mornings of three generations of children as TV's Captain Kangaroo. Now, this award winning performer offers heartwarming and practical advice on raising well-adjusted, happy children as he shares his thoughts on a wide range of topics—from the importance of your child's self-esteem to the challenges of parenting today.

__FOODS FOR HEALTHY KIDS by Dr. Lendon Smith
0-425-09276-3/$4.50
Dr. Lendon Smith, America's leading authority on nutrition for children, tells how to prevent and alleviate health problems such as asthma, allergies, depression, constipation, hyperactivity, sleep problems and tension—not with medicine, but with good, nourishing food. He gives you his total nutrition program, complete with more than 100 recipes.

__LEARNINGAMES FOR THE FIRST THREE YEARS
Joseph Sparling & Isabelle Lewis 0-425-08847-2/$4.50
This book includes 100 fully-illustrated easy and fun adult-child games. All are designed to combine loving, playing and learning in an effective program that will enrich your child's life.

For Visa, MasterCard and American Express orders ($15 minimum) call: 1-800-631-8571

FOR MAIL ORDERS: CHECK BOOK(S). FILL OUT COUPON. SEND TO:

BERKLEY PUBLISHING GROUP
390 Murray Hill Pkwy., Dept. B
East Rutherford, NJ 07073

NAME_____
ADDRESS_____
CITY_____
STATE _____ ZIP_____
PLEASE ALLOW 6 WEEKS FOR DELIVERY.
PRICES ARE SUBJECT TO CHANGE WITHOUT NOTICE.

POSTAGE AND HANDLING:
$1.75 for one book, 75¢ for each additional. Do not exceed $5.50.

BOOK TOTAL $ _____
POSTAGE & HANDLING $ _____
APPLICABLE SALES TAX $ _____
(CA, NJ, NY, PA)
TOTAL AMOUNT DUE $ _____

PAYABLE IN US FUNDS.
(No cash orders accepted.)